I0081311

WHAT ABOUT FATHERS?

FAMILY LAW; GENDER & RACIAL BIAS

BY

COLLEEN DAVIS

Copyright 2020 by Colleen Davis

ISBN: 978-1-7359834-0-0

All rights reserved. This book or parts thereof may not be reproduced in any form, stored in any retrieval system, or transmitted in any form by any means, electronic, mechanical, photocopy, recording, or otherwise, without prior written permission of the publisher, except as provided by United States of America copyright law.

This biography is based on a true story. To protect the innocent and guilty, I have tried to recreate events, locales, and conversations from my memories of them, data given to me, and permission to use the data by PW Davis from whom permitted me to write his biography. To maintain their anonymity, I have changed the names of individuals and places. I have also changed some identifying characteristics and details such as physical properties, occupations, and places of residence.

I would like to thank the real-life members of the family portrayed in this book for taking me into their home and accepting me as one of their own. I recognize that their memories of the events described in this book are different than my own. They are each fine, decent, and hard-working people. The book was not intended to hurt the family. Both my publisher and I regret any unintentional harm resulting from the publishing and marketing of this book, *What About The Fathers? Family Law; Gender & Racial Bias.*

Table of Contents

INTRODUCTION 1

CHAPTER 1 FAMILY LIFE AND THE MOTHER'S DEMISE 5

CHAPTER 2 THE HOMELESS SHELTER 22

CHAPTER 3 PRESTON DRIVE 26

CHAPTER 4 WHERE'S "THE" ONE-MARGARITAVILLE-WIFE #2 33

CHAPTER 5 CELEBACY 40

CHAPTER 6 MEETING "THE" ONE.. 46

CHAPTER 7 GENDER INEQUALITY AND RACISM 58

CHAPTER 8 CHILD SUPPORT HANDBOOKS VS REALITY 75

CHAPTER 9 PSYCHOLOGY OF ABANDONED CHILDREN 82

CHAPTER 10 FAMILY INCIDENTS AUG 2019-CURRENT 90

CHAPTER 11 CONTINUOUS FIGHT.. 131

INTRODUCTION

This biography intends to tell one single black father's story. There are tremendous single mothers out there doing everything for their children with little to no support and we commend you for your sacrifices. This is a never-ending story of perseverance, strength, and a deep love for family. Patrick Wayne Davis, known as PW, immediately told Colleen he was a proud single father of his four children, ages fourteen through ten. The first thought that came to my mind was, "How in God's name does a single black father in a racially divided nation and bias court system get awarded as the primary residential parent for all four of his children?" Also, culturally, a deeply engrained perception exists that mothers are more nurturing, and fathers simply reside in their roles as a provider.

We have only heard stories of deadbeat dads dropping seeds and bailing or rich fathers who never spend time with their children and leave the single mothers to struggle, knowing they do not have the financial means to hire an attorney to fight them in court to enforce court-ordered child support. Being the inquisitive, non-judgmental person who has a deep calling to fight for what is right, Colleen was compelled to share his story and the multifaceted battle he faces every single day as a single black father, loving family man, and dedicated provider of security and safety for his family. Who is he? He is not what is portrayed in the media as a dead-beat dad, no job, pants sagging, weed head, low riding car portrayal of a black man. He is confident with a smile, wears wranglers, drives a Chevy pickup, and loves learning about history.

His dedication to his career as an electrician of over 20 years earned him the title of Superintendent, which is rare for a black man in a predominantly white good old boys club. His love of travel takes him and the family on road trips to new places to make new memories. Instead of looking back through thousands of pictures on his phone to reminisce, he spends time creating homemade scrapbooks. It is meaningful to him, to know his grandchildren will look at the scrapbooks and say "wow, you went to a lot of cool places." Also, he chooses specific pictures, gets an 8x10 print made, puts the picture in a frame, and hangs them up on his travel wall in the dining room. He loves to joke around, remains humble, tells the truth, and predicts the outcomes of people's lives based on their choices, even when most people do not want to hear it. When PW is ready to make a point, his opening line begins with "Here's the deal." Most of all he loves his family deep within his soul. He has and will do everything to fight for them within a deeply rooted racially and gender bias family law and child support system which typically awards children to the biological mother. Intrigued yet?

You are invited to listen to his stories with an open mind and heart through the lens of PW, which will shed light and help other fathers fight for their families in a racially and gender bias child support system rooted in old laws and lack of enforcement. Colleen is grateful to PW for bringing me into his family to share life and for sharing his life's journey with honesty and humbleness. Never has she met a man with such a positive outlook on life in dire circumstances and who continues to be shackled by the bureaucracy of the child support and justice system.

CHAPTER 1 FAMILY LIFE AND THE MOTHER'S DEMISE

PW was in his early twenties when he met the future mother of his children in California while on vacation. They were both attending a college football game. In a chance meeting at a concession stand, it felt like fate. They started talking quite a bit and began to make a connection. After a couple of months, and two visits later in November, they had gotten pregnant. Deep down he knew this was not the woman he wanted to marry, yet what was he to do in this situation. He talked to his parents about the situation he had gotten himself in. His mother, being blunt as usual, said, "Do not marry that girl if she cannot be trusted and you are not in love with her," and his father advised him to do the right thing and marry her. In the short time they had been talking, her behavior seemed secretive and stories were not adding up.

He decided to follow his father's advice and make a go of it with his new family life. They decided to have her move to

Tennessee, and they got married. As he got to know his new wife, he did his best to support her through her challenges with her past. In short, she comes from a long history of being exposed to drugs, alcoholism, and overall toxic co-dependent family members. They are masters at working the system to receive benefits for free and only come around to each other to borrow money from each other, that they have no intention of paying back. Whenever the mother comes across extra money the family comes out of the woodwork to see what they can sponge off her, then when the money runs out, they disappear like cockroaches. Initially, people may feel empathy for her for what she has been through, yet there are lots of other people who have been through far worse and don't choose to make it normal behavior to manipulate and take advantage of others their entire life, including her children.

Though their marriage was going through some normal ups and downs, what PW experienced surpassed the usual. He did what he thought he was supposed to do for the family, work hard, provide security, and make them feel safe. PW is a generous gift giver and expresses his love by surprise flowers, gifts, and small tokens to make his loved ones feel special. To prepare for Christmas, he worked extra hours to ensure they got the gifts they wanted. One year, he got his wife a diamond necklace, his daughter a pair of fancy boots and the boys received the latest gaming equipment and new laptops. He is not a man of regret, though reflecting on how much he gave his family, ended up spoiling them. His wife pawned the $5,000 wedding band set and diamond necklace and the kids lost their possessions in the storage unit.

The reason they lost their belongings in the storage unit, was because she was supposed to be paying the bills yet chose to spend the money elsewhere. He supported his wife's dreams of going into the medical field, bought her a new Jeep, and worked more hours to keep the house going so could fulfill her dreams. After the birth of their last son, things took a toxic turn. Some women experience postpartum depression, yet instead of addressing the issues, which can be managed, she chose to start cheating on PW multiple times and would leave the children for long periods and even for a week to go be with other men. PW stated she had a hysterectomy and things got worse after she healed up from her surgery. Her issues were deep-rooted and not solely related to a hysterectomy or depression. Her drinking and partying got out of control and she would leave the children by themselves for long periods.

In a personal letter written in August 2016, PW knew their marriage was on thin ice. "I was not able to sleep for months. My boys hung on me and begged me to make mommy stop getting stop so mad and some nights wetting the bed being so upset. Most nights I would wake up with all four kids sleeping with me in a tiny twin bed. I was a little selfish. I will come to terms with leaving because of my fear of going to jail for no reason, it happens to the "black males" all the time. So, first, I told my kids that I love them and my daughter that I am sorry I could not be there for her birthday this year. I told her daddy had to go out of town to work for a week, which was not true. All the kids cried and begged me not to go. I also told them to love each other and remember who you are. I also told them if your mom leaves you alone, call the police and say your mom has been gone for 24 hours and that I am working out of town. But all I could think about is how she would lie to the police and court system to get the order of protection. This was the first-time plan that I came up with.

I was going to leave for a week, knowing she would be drinking and doing things with men and leave the kids. This would show the police and court systems she is an unfit mother. Of course, she was laying in the bed next to me half-drunk. With all of the stuff she had put me and the kids through, I still wanted to hold her and tell her I love her, but I knew deep down we were done because alcohol, drugs, and men were taking control of her life. So, I packed my things and got halfway down the road and got to thinking, what is she gets drunk, passes out and some guy over there takes advantage of my daughter and hurts my boys. I turned around and came right back home."

When they lived in Atoka, down the road from PW's parents, the mother had him falsely arrested in front of the kids and his parents for domestic violence. To prove the case that the laws and court system favor white women, half of the domestic cases police respond to are not legit, stated a police officer who was the husband of a former co-worker of Colleen's. The mother had come home that night drunk and stumbling and ready to argue. She entered the home and started yelling at PW for working so much, then she stumbled, fell backward, and hit the back of her head on a coffee table. PW was trying to help her up and she started to hit him and called him a "lazy no good nigger." He had to hold her to keep her from throwing punches at him. She broke free and ran to the bathroom where she called her mother in Missouri.

PW's mother in law dialed 911 from Missouri and told the police that PW was beating her. They were in cahoots together because they knew PW had custody of the kids. The cops showed up, he explained himself, the kids told the officer she came home drunk and PW told them the truth that she slipped and hit the back of her head on the coffee table. Isn't it odd that a supposed domestic violent man would hit someone on the back of the head and has custody of all four of their children? The office said, either you go to jail, you both go to jail or I call social services. PW said my parents are right down the road, we can take the kids there" and before you know it PW was in handcuffs falsely accused of domestic violence. The police officer said he smelled liquor on her breath, and she lied and told them she was not drinking. He got released later the next day and came home to a wife still lying in bed hungover.

In the courtroom, she let her emotions take over and said she would not have to come home drunk all the time if he would show more respect for her as a woman. The judge ripped her up and down for lying under oath, yet the punishment ended there. PW stated that the assistant district attorney was eager to throw the book at him. The judge told her, "I know you are doing your job and you want cases closed quickly, however, Miss Davis lied under oath. The day after next, he found a lawyer he could afford and got the charges dropped.

The judge deemed him innocent. However, PW must pay $400 to get the incident expunged off his record to the court system, even though he was innocent. The fee remains unpaid because he does not have the financial means to pay for it. It is a common strategy used by the justice system to avoid potential lawsuits for individuals who have been wrongly accused through the fault of the court system if a lesser charge or plea bargain is agreed upon. She got a slap on the hand for filing a fake police report. PW was in a no-win situation. If he were to defend himself against the punches, he is considered an aggressive black male and if he stands there and takes it, he is a weak man or getting beat up by a woman.

PW caught her in the act with other men many times and had to document each incident, even though it tore him up inside. He wondered how the mother of our children can destroy our family like this. Other indiscretions involved the kids getting free snacks at the school because she was involved with the janitor and a member of the congregation. The straw that broke the camel's back was when she had 2 months of school left, had decided to quit school, because of one of many a man she was involved with told her to do so. PW had to pay back over $40,000 because she decided to listen to others and not do what is right. He always told her to be a leader and not listen to other people and the influence of others led her to the decision to quit. Every incident PW documented helped him become the custodial parent of his four children. Since the mother was living so recklessly, he knew she was not going to create a stable environment for them. In October 2016, at their Madison, TN address, PW dispatched police. Upon arrival, PW stated that his wife who had split from him over a month ago was with suspect #2 left with their four children and was proceeding to move to Missouri.

PW stated that he received phone calls from his wife asking for money to which he has been refusing to give her, due to the possibility of drug habits by suspect #2. PW stated that he is in the process of getting a divorce from his wife and he would like information on how to obtain an order of protection against her for him and his children. PW stated the reasoning behind him wishing to obtain an order of protection is due to her making repeated phone calls for money and harassing him about money. PW also stated that he had seen a suspicious black SUV driving by the residence and observed a black male, suspect #2, and was told: "he had better give them kids back to the mother."

PW felt intimidated at that point and proceeded to Madison precinct on the night of the report to make a report of the occurrences. He stated that no acts of physical violence had been committed and that he did not wish to be taken to a safe alternative location with his children. He was provided with information on counseling for him and his children and was advised on how to obtain an order of protection. Extra patrols were assigned to the area for protection. In late October 2016, a petition was filed for Order of Protection by PW for two reasons.

On March 3rd, 2017, both parties went to court and were instructed to get a divorce. After court, the mother went straight to the children's school and acted violently to the point where the school staff had to call the police. The mother and the kids were detained, and the plan was for her to take the children out of state. She had walked away for 11 months. Metro police told her since she had not been in their lives, they are giving the children back to PW.

After this, she started calling PW from several different numbers and devices threatening him. She said, "I'm going to get your black fucking ass and those two bitches from the Salvation Army." After a phone call, a black male called PW and stated I better give the children black to her or he was going to come and get him. During the initial incident in early October, with the same guy, she ransacked their current place, stole electronics, emptied the safe, bank accounts, and filed a false tax return, and stole $10,000. She was supposed to be running the house finances and failed to pay many bills, including their storage unit.

This day was the biggest loss to PW were the baby pictures of his children that he will never get back. She raided their home while the kids were in school and PW as at work. The only reason he knew about it, was that a neighbor called him and told him about his wife and a strange male going in and out of his home. PW raced home and did not make it in time. He dropped to his knees, prayed for strength, for he had lost so much.

The gun incident on October 21st, 2016 was the most significant and threatening of all. At the Preston Drive address, PW filed a report for trespassing. She had brought an unknown black male to the house and the male proceeded to say that he was going to shoot this house up and kill everybody in there. At this point, Miss Davis and the black male had traveled there many times between 12m-2am. She was driving a red car and she stopped, and the young black male got out of the vehicle with what looked like an AR-15 rifle. It was difficult to see the exact type of gun. PW woke the kids up and ran out the back door.

Here is where the non-enforcement of law failed to protect the innocent. This experience was traumatic to the children and they are mentally exhausted. Miss Davis took a plea bargain since she did not have the gun in her possession. The angels were on PW's side that night. A neighbor from across the street was coming home from working his shift and was able to get a videotape of the incident and turned the evidence into the police. She was ordered to not see the children for 6 months and chose to be in and out of their lives for around 11 months. Even though she had an order of protection against her, which clearly states she is to not come to the residence to drop off the children, she chose to show up a day early for a drop off on one of her visitations.

PW stated that during an argument ensued by Miss Davis, had their four children for visitation and was supposed to have them until tomorrow, yet showed up with them at their residence today. PW advised that he did not approve of this because he was about to go out of town for the night and Miss Davis is not even supposed to bring the kids to his residence according to the parenting agreement. He stated they are supposed to meet in a neutral area. Miss Davis said the only reason she brought the kids back early is that they asked her to do so. Miss Davis was advised not to come back to Mr. Davis's residence at his request.

The comment made by Miss Davis regarding the Salvation Army led him to a financial rock bottom for the family. They were forced to live in a hotel for a month and by the grace of God, the Salvation Army had room for PW and his children. PW had no other options for the money, so he decided to go to a pawn shop and sell his power tools. All those years and hard-earned money to build up his tools were wiped out in an instant, yet he had to save his family and keep them safe. The only thing he kept was hands tools. Tools are an electrician's bread and butter. It takes years to build up an electrician's tool base and he is still trying to recover one tool at a time, because of his limited budget.

The most disheartening part about the aftermath is that the children are in complete denial and blame their father for everything and remain in a rollercoaster state of confusion not understanding the sacrifices he made and still makes every day to ensure their safety and security. The major reason for the hatred is the filth and lies the mother constantly tells the children. Cornbread accused his father of taking his $10 years ago, which is not true. His assumption comes from his mother who told him the child support she pays goes to spoiling your stepmom and he is stealing from you. JC teased Colleen about PW working late, asking her, "How do you know he is not cheating on you?" Where else is a 13-year-old going to drum up crazy ideas? Colleen responded in her non-sugar-coating way and said" I know he is not cheating because we trust and love one another very much."

The mother has and will go to great lengths to create a wedge in his marriage. Her strategy is to use the children to obtain information and spend energy trying to destroy what she

chose to abandon years ago. She holds on to resentment,

unknowingly she has for herself and spews hate towards the

father of her children. He often tells Colleen they are lost and

walk all over me. Colleen agrees and reassures him that deep

down they care, though are covered up by years of verbal abuse

and abandonment by their mother. She has them so brainwashed

and manipulated that their heads are in the clouds about nearly

everything, continue to disrespect him, yet come back to reality

at times. They do not have gratitude and remain ungrateful to

the man that saved them. He is noticed in the older boys that

they are having moments where they are trying to figure things

out. PW shows them how to do things around the house and

they love checking out the progress of the garden.

There was a moment where PW asked them if they

wanted to live with their mother and Cornbread had a facial

expression of "ya right" as almost as if he knew she was not

capable of proving what he needed. There is a high possibility they will become a product of the toxic generational epigenetic machine and repeat the cycle. He can work 90 hours, take them on beach vacations, buy cool clothes, yet all of that is erased in a moment by a rubber ball that the mother buys them from a Walmart vending machine.

CHAPTER 2 THE HOMELESS SHELTER

Since his situation is rare, there are no programs in place for single black fathers facing such dire circumstances for themselves and their families. He had enough money to get them a hotel room to start. When they were at the hotel, PW would stop by Dollar Tree and buy as much as he could afford of $1 microwavable meals. He often went hungry himself, so his kids had a meal for the night. During their stay at the hotel, the mother never contributed a penny for their needs, instead, she called the cops on him and told the authorities that he had four minors living in a hotel and it was unsafe, towards the end of their stay. The visit from the police got them kicked out of the hotel, even though they were ok, and the hotel was paid for.

After a couple of months of living in a hotel with what money he was able to earn each week after he had everything stolen from him, the Salvation Army notified him of one room left for him and his four children to stay at. In a letter dated March 3rd, 2017, he had a sign of relief of this blessing and knew it was the next step for him getting back on his feet for his family. They had been accepted into the Salvation Army Transitional Housing Unit. Typically, shelters are for single mothers as are more programs for them, in general, to raise their children solo, especially when the other parent is not being supportive. PW knew God was on his side when he got the news about the space in the homeless shelter.

He did his best to make things feel as normal as possible for the kids. They had curfews and rules to follow, yet it was a place to stay in the interim until he figured things out. A community kitchen shared with strangers enabled them to cook some of their meals by scratch. Temporary food stamps were available, which provided more nutritious meals for them and a better night's sleep. To take their minds off things, they played dominos at night, watched movies, and became experts at playing spades. He had a spa night with his daughter, and they put on face masks for fun. There were many nights where he had to hold his youngest son until he fell asleep from being scared and crying. He was too small to understand what his mother had done to the family and why this was not discussed because the information was too big to handle for a young child.

PW had fallen into a funk after one month of being in the shelter. He started asking himself what he had done wrong to cause this situation and felt depressed. The dedication, love, and effort he put into his marriage crushed his heart, for he loved her. He said his kids encouraged him to get up and go to work and expressed they were sad to see him sad. This was the spark he needed to pull himself back out of his depression. He still went to work, donated plasma, and on breaks called anyone he could think of to see if they knew of a place they can rent. His credit was trashed by his ex-wife, so he had to find a friend of a friend type deal. He needed to find a desperate homeowner who had a home that was not in perfect condition and was dead weight.

The goal was to establish a true sense of home. The children had been through so much and needed a soft place to land and call home. When he reflects on the days of the shelter, he is eternally grateful for the two women, which includes his caseworker who helped him obtain temporary residence, gave him motivation and understanding to help him see a bright future for him and his family. After numerous calls, PW had a buddy of his tell him about a house for rent that needed some minor repairs, was vacant, affordable and they could move in immediately.

This was the breakthrough that he needed to establish security for his family. The sad part about it was he received no help for the children from his ex-wife. She ran off to Missouri with some random dude with all their money even though she has court-ordered child support payments. He was left to fight for his family by his means. PW is a fight for what's right for his family, so he pressed on doing what he had to do to get all of them into a new place.

CHAPTER 3 PRESTON DRIVE

The last few nights in the shelter felt bittersweet and long. They had been through so much as a family and the anticipation of a new home was exciting. They packed up what little things they had left, loaded up the Chevy pickup, and headed to their new place. PW had saved up enough money for two months' rent and a security deposit. His lease was part verbal and partially handwritten on notebook paper in an agreement with an unknown slumlord. PW had the intention of buying the property in a few years and from what knowledge he had of the place, the repairs appeared to be moderate. He left work early one day and did a quick walkthrough and decided this will be the place where he and his family can start life over in a new way. They gathered their things and drove over to the new home.

When they walked in, cockroaches scurried around and the place in massive groups and the place had become infested with all types of bugs. The kids got scared and freaked out over the sight of bugs. PW immediately called the landlord and told him about this situation and the war began. The landlord refused to take care of the situation and told PW that he signed an "as is" lease and it was his responsibility to rectify the insect infestation. Money was tight, he needed to feed the kids, though in his problem-solving fashion found an exterminator to come the next day and destroy the insects.

They got a cheap hotel for the night until the chemicals had time to dissipate out of the air. He left the children at the hotel that afternoon and went to donate plasma, so they could have a meal for the night. The next day they were able to move in and got settled into their new home. Princess and JC got their rooms, Cornbread and KK shared a bunk bed in the backroom by the laundry area. Unfortunately, the home did not come with appliances.

Through others' generosity, he received a refrigerator, washer, and dryer. He came up with the money to purchase a stove and microwave. The other significant issue was the HVAC system. The age of the system and lack of repairs made it inoperable. They had moved into the home during the fall and the wintertime was soon approaching. At the end of September, he had saved up enough money through plasma donations and was able to afford multiple floor heaters.

Each of his children had their heater for their rooms and the other two were placed in the kitchen and living room. Additionally, the home had not been maintained and was not energy efficient. Several windows were partially broken throughout the home and filth everywhere. The combination of the windows, poor insulation, and floor heaters drove the electricity bill up to $400-$500 per month. Since he has a moderately good paying job, though still broke, he is considered too rich to qualify for electricity programs or food stamps.

PW must live in a constant state of making sure everything is according to Child Protective Services guidelines. If there is food in the refrigerator the children do not feel like eating, they can tell their mother there is nothing to eat and she will make a phone call for CPS to make an unannounced home visit. PW is required to have beds, furniture, clean clothes, and security. He added more debt to his financial burden by having to finance large pieces of furniture and being forced to choose weekly payment plans for affordability and because of his poor credit score that his ex-wife trashed while they were married.

The Preston drive home became their special place for almost three years. PW had to get up early to work far away in Nashville each day and JC the oldest, whom PW put in charge, making sure his sister and brothers got up and were ready for school each day. He shouldered tremendous responsibility at a young age. Now 13, he gets up around 6 am, makes himself coffee, breakfast, and watches YouTube videos, sort of a routine an adult man may have.

Often, PW had to work late, and none of the children told him the milk was out. He would get home after a long day and would then have to go back out to pick up a few items. He always had enough food in the house for them to have sandwiches, snacks, and breakfast. On days where he had more time to plan dinners, his menu includes chicken enchiladas, burgers or sausage, and dirty rice. Often after a hard day's work, which is physically demanding, he came home to a house that looked like a bomb had been dropped. The kitchen sink was overflowing with dishes and he had to cook their dinner.

They ate dinner as late as 9:30 pm on school nights and he had to help them with their homework and fill out extensive school packets. He was holding it down the best he could, being a single black father. They learned from their mother to hate their dad and none of them took initiative to help around the house, a behavior pattern that is a work in progress today. The only time things got done was when he called them when he was about 30 minutes out. He created a fire drill to get them to clean. They respond to him getting on them with intensity versus understanding he has worked a 10-hour day, feels exhausted, and how much it would mean if they could learn to be a team player.

With their mom in their life pumping their minds with negativity, he knew they will never change. They were a perfectly imperfect family, who had suffered lots of trauma, took trips, still had fun, and we're conditioned to interact how they do, even though their love is covered up by self-destructive behavior. They spent nights watching movies, playing spades and dominos. No one cared if they had to move the pile of clean laundry off the table to play games. As Princess got older, her girlfriends would come over and giggle into the later hours of the night. Even on a super tight income, he fed his daughter's friends without hesitation.

PW takes great pride in providing for his family, which he says is a given and not something a hero does. The back and forth with the crazy landlord became normal for PW. He had to run over to Navy Federal and deposit the rent in cash into his landlord's account. He always kept his receipts, because the landlord's wife was crazy. She spent the money fast and PW would get aggressive texts from his landlord accusing him of not paying rent. Also, the agreement was to pay half of the water bill each month, which also had to be deposited into his landlord's bank account. The last three months in the place were a constant battle. The landlord was in a financial crisis and was pressuring PW to take care of the repairs in the home.

Eventually, PW got an estimate of the repairs from a contractor, which added up to around $50,000. There is no way he had the financial means to take on any of the repairs. He was not even able to afford enough food to stock up the food pantry. The plumbing started to fail and there was a trickle of water for them to take showers in. Eventually, through God's will and synchronicity, he and the kids were able to move into a new home through the efforts of whom will become his third wife and true love.

CHAPTER 4 WHERE'S "THE" ONE-MARGARITAVILLE-WIFE #2

Where does a single father of four children find real long-lasting love? He describes himself as a family man and says he is happy surrounded by his loved ones, food on the table, and having a roof over our heads. Our current culture is filled with an easy out mentality and social media saturates our minds with sexualized images of what makes a healthy relationship. In other words, if we do not like a minor flaw in someone we can move on to the next person. He is not advocating staying in a toxic relationship or with someone for who you are not a match. Both genders are at fault. Men are running around dating multiple women, getting tail, as well as women being Golddiggers and being manipulative. It makes things extremely difficult for those of us who desire a real healthy relationship to find a partner who is right for us and will be there through the storms too.

One must not give up on finding real love and when faced with a one-hit-wonder, move on quickly, because we teach people how to treat us when we choose to stay and put up with their mistreatment. He clearly states it is difficult to find a partner who rides out the high and lows of what life throws at us. He endured tremendous trauma, heartache in his marriage to the mother of his four children yet stayed faithful and dedicated hoping she may choose to come out of her darkness and turn her life around. How much one is supposed to endure is their personal choice and for him, the safety of his children meant more to him than staying with a woman who did not want to be with him. Due to PW's hectic work schedule and trips to the plasma bank to donate, he chose to go online and see what the possibilities were. Like many people experience, he got sucked into an endless amount of random dates and potential partners looking to "have fun" and not looking for anything serious. He has always been upfront about being a single black father of four children.

Some women are confused as to why he is the custodial parent while others did not care. One person, in particular, told him to tell the kids to shut up while they were on the phone and that they were too much to handle. His response to that was, "This is my life and I come with all of it. Either you are in or not." He met a woman with a Ph.D. who worked at a museum. They seemed to connect, though whenever he asked her to go on a dinner date, she made up excuses or always said she had other plans. Come to find out, she was embarrassed to be seen with a blue-collar worker, who was also African American. PW immediately cut ties.

He knew it was going to take an extra-strong woman to hold the home down with him, a true queen. The home is crazy and wild, and they did not get the nurturing from a true loving strong woman. In general, society is conditioned to think females are the sole nurturer and often feel puzzled a mother is capable of so much destruction. Keep in mind the children have been through trauma and have not had a sense of stability from a mother or mother figure to give the guidance and boundaries that they need to know.

It became difficult for him to go on dates because he has no family in Clarksville to ask to babysit them and it is hard to find a sitter who can handle the family dynamics for the night. Deep down they are great kids, covered up by layers of dysfunctional behavior learned from their trauma and mother who fills their minds with broken promises and keeps their heads in the clouds. When they get riled up, they yell, fight, dance, and become wild. He loves his children and will continue to do anything to keep them safe. In the same breath, he knows they will have to fall flat on their face one day and may come running back to him when they understand their mother will choose to use them like she has used so many people in her life. He never gave up on love and did his best to navigate online dating sites and started talking to a woman from Alabama, when he was in the shelter with the kids.

The conversation flowed well, and they continued to get to know one another. She made trips to visit all of them in the shelter and after PW got settled in the Preston Drive home, they decided she would move to Clarksville and start a life together. Since she was from another state, it took a couple of months for her to get her nursing license in Tennessee. During this time, PW supported the family, including his wife. They decided to flip a house together and broke even and he genuinely believed she loved him because she made a huge effort to visit them in a homeless shelter.

Her license got approved and she began working as a nurse putting in a lot of hours. The money she made went to her grown children's college and did not support her current family. Though by law she is not obligated to help with the kids, PW felt some support would be greatly appreciated. Soon after their marriage, she started to slip up and show signs of her drinking habits. During family road trips she had to be half tanked up and one day PW and Cornbread decided to surprise her and detail her car while she was sleeping. Low and behold, when they cleaned under the seats, they found a huge stash of 50 ml hard liquor bottles under the seat. He confronted her about the booze, and she yelled at him and said, "I have a lot of stress at my job and it helps me numb the pain when you have seen a child die on your shift". Granted the stress of being a nurse is intense though he knew she was an alcoholic. They went out to a Mexican restaurant one evening as a family. She ordered the largest margarita on the menu, ended up getting smashed at dinner, and later in the evening puked and passed out. A couple of months went by and PW decided to quit his job and find another one. The stress with his current role made him endure 90-hour work weeks and he had become burnt out. The company required him to work tremendous overtime and told him, you either keep up or find something else. He was only off for two weeks and the whole time his wife nagged him about finding a job and forgot his support he gave her when she had to wait for her license to get approved and it was no big deal to him.

Often, he caught her secretly texting in the bathroom or their bedroom. He confronted her and she finally fessed up she was talking to multiple exes. He shook his head in frustration, for again he chose a woman who he thought loved him as much as he loved her. Lastly, the craziest part of the situation is the mother of the children harassed her and made her life hell through texts, phone calls, and Facebook. PW had warned her, that his ex-wife was crazy and will pretend she is your friend, yet inside wants to create a wedge in the marriage. Strangely, both of his wives became friends with each other, even after the harassment.

PW attributed this friendship to "like attracts like" Eventually the two women had a huge fight and were no longer friends. This was the last straw for him, and he decided to get the marriage annulled. Again, he was on his own, which he was accustomed to, though he deeply wanted a wife, best friend, and strong mother figure for his children and live life together in harmony instead of chaos.

CHAPTER 5 CELEBACY

After his divorce from his second wife, a couple of months later he decided to try going online to see if you could make a decent connection with a true queen. The stakes were different this time. He spent some time reading, researching, and tapping into his relationship with God to see if there was something else, he could do for himself to attract a woman he desired. He took a vow of celibacy for six months and this included not pleasing himself either. In a world where you can get a sexual partner as quickly as pizza delivery, he chose to view his body as a temple in hopes of putting the positive intention out there to attract a real partner.

With all the dating apps, swiping right, swiping left, celibacy was a game-changer for him and certainly changed the conversations on the dates he had. According to Rumi, "Your task is not to seek love, but merely to seek and find all the barriers within yourself that you have built against it." He felt when you stopped searching, you are no longer focused on an outcome and you begin to live with more intention. Dating can become a distraction for loneliness and at times he went all in searching for a result. He worked in Nashville and went on several dates and told himself if he saw one sign from a first date where the woman had the behavior of those in the past, he was out immediately, no second date.

One woman was obsessed with politics and religion, which was the main topic of their first date conversation. PW, like he always does, calls out the truth which people do not like to hear on topics. The woman got in a huff and started a heated argument because of his comments. They both went their separate ways, then 2 days later, she apologized and invited him over for a home-cooked meal. PW agreed to a second date and let her know his choice of celibacy. She seemed to be ok with his decision and still invited him over. Excited for a home-cooked meal, he arrived at her home on a Saturday night.

When he arrived, he got greeted at the door with a smile, and an apology, because she had not even gone to the store or started dinner. Shaking his head in disappointment, he left and, on the way, out, she ran after him and said, "We can order some pizza and watch a movie." He proceeded to leave, and never speak to her again. On the first date, she started an argument that was familiar to him from his past relationships, and on the second date, she had no intention of making a meal, which he knew to see the red flags of one's words compared to actions. Someone of her nature is not a great fit for a wife or a mother figure for his four children. After a few dates with some hipster women in Nashville, PW started talking to another woman, who was highly educated, and they made an instant connection. They went on several dates and each time bonded a little more. Then one day, she had not reached out in a couple of days. PW decided to hit her up and she said, "Oh I have been busy with my cousin in town."

He had no problem with that and said, "Have fun with your family" and left things with that. Then the next day, he happened to be at a park with the kids and he saw her in the distance, hugging a man and kissing him on the cheek. Even though one day he wanted her to meet his kids, this was not the right time. He gave the kids money to go get ice cream and he approached her. She had already said goodbye to the other man before he came up to her. PW asked her about what he saw and she said "Oh, that's my brother and sister in law" Puzzled, PW said, "So which is it?" She broke down and explained that it was her husband. They had been married for a while and he had gotten back from Afghanistan and she was taking care of him yet was eventually going to leave him. Even though PW was glad she finally told him the truth, he did not want to put himself in that position. He also asked her if she slept with him and she was honest and said she did.

The trial and error of dating continued, yet he never gave up on finding a woman who would love him and the kids unconditionally. When one decides to be celibate, spiritually, self-awareness heightens and personal growth occurs, which in turn puts a stronger positive vibe in the world to attract whom you are meant to be with. Also, sex is sacred, and the body is s

temple. Sex is fun at the moment and it is incredible to get your

rocks off, yet long term makes most people feel lonely and

disconnected. At the beginning of this journey, he admitted the

first couple weeks were the toughest, because he is a man with

strong sexual drive, yet as time went on, he began to focus on

himself on a deeper level. The desire to marry his best friend and

a strong woman almost seemed impossible to him, given what he

had been through.

He expressed his actions of choosing women which took

so much from him was also his responsibility too. Why was he

attracting women who had low self-esteem and needed saving?

When he went to court for his divorce from the mother's

children, a counselor helped him figure out why he kept

repeating the patterns. He knew taking the initiative to learn

more about these situations would also help his court case too.

Since he is a black single male, he is already judged by society and

the court system which favors white females. The counselor led him to discover that his near-death car accident in high school conditioned him to save females because he was not able to save his girlfriend from dying. He does not remember the accident, yet his mind developed a defense mechanism to fix broken women. His eyes and mind were wide open, and he vowed to never choose a woman who had the previous personality traits of his ex-wives.

During this time, deep down he knows he deserves better and a woman who is willing to take on the role of a mother to his four children, work through the challenges and enjoy the fun times too. The perfect woman for him needed to be strong-willed, come from a healthy family and have her own goals going on. Most of all, she must love and value herself and meet him in a place where they are self-aware and able to grow with each other and have a relationship with God.

CHAPTER 6 MEETING "THE" ONE

PW decided to go on a dating app for interracial dating in June of 2019. He admitted that he saw Colleen's profile, known as wonderwoman11 and he swiped by it, then came back to it. He had a preconceived notion that she was high maintenance, especially living in Chicago. Then a voice in his head said, go for it, I have nothing to lose. Here is how the initial conversation went.

PW: Good morning beautiful. I know I am not in your age group, but I'd be a damn fool not to try to talk to such a pretty girl and try to get to know better. My name is PW age 38, a single father of four, divorced 6 years, lives in Clarksville, Tennessee, just outside of Nashville. I work as an electrician for the past 20 years. Just trying to spark up a friendship and see if it leads to something and it's a win-win for me.

Colleen: Well I am more interested in a person's character. What does PW stand for? I have friends that are single parents, great ones. Electrical is a great skill. Colleen is my name

PW: Well Colleen, I am glad that you are looking for someone's character. I'll tell you what PW stands for when we get to know each other a little better in a friendship. I'm looking for a down ass chick and that down ass friend. Not looking to rush anything, always up for fun, just get to know me a little better and I promise you, you will not be disappointed.

Colleen: That's cool Mr. TN

PW: Thank God. Some are thirsty or they're the opposite and don't want to get to know you

Colleen: LOL, I'm a badass in a good way

PW: That's what's up

Colleen: It's genetic

PW: Well that's good, cuz I don't want to talk to someone boring. I'm like the kid who can go do some crazy shit, not jail shit, just want to live my life when I am freed up from my children

Colleen: I'm the most misunderstood person ever, I'm a free spirit, but very loyal

PW: Yeah I don't want you to kind of take being buck wild as being thuggish too. I just like to have fun like you, like you said a free spirit

Colleen: I don't want to bring bad karma to myself! I'm a good kind of random crazy. Most people are boring. I'm a lady, though I'm not reserved. I've gotta be who I am.

PW: Cool, here's my number

     From the beginning, he felt a deep bond like no other and Colleen continued to act and be herself with no games. Her energy was so strong, PW talked to her the whole time he was on vacation as the designated driver with some buddies in The Gulf Shores. He was surrounded by the youngest and finest women wanting to give their tail up to him, yet he became so intrigued that he was blind to the meat market around him. At one point on his trip, his buddies threatened to throw his clothes and suitcase in the pool if he did not join them. He finally hung out with them and began to show Colleen off to those around him. Of course, he got the "you gonna bang that" comments, however, he was beginning to fall in love with her. When they were hungover, he went to the zoo, checked out some aircraft carriers, and talked to Colleen the whole time, and sent her pictures. It was as if she was on vacation with him. When he got back to Clarksville, it would be a couple more days before his children got back from visiting the aunt in Texas. They talked several times a time and continued to connect. To express how much he loved her, he wrote her daily love letters.

Letter #1

I never knew I could love anyone as much as I do love you and always was my give to myself away like this. I never thought I'd find someone to love so unconditionally Colleen, I found that person to live with forever and most happily

Letter #2

What a day where do I start my beautiful Queen!!!! On how amazing you are. I can let you know I'm needy and spoiled by you. You are a real woman who knows how to treat a man right and I cannot wait to make love to you. Friday won't get here soon enough. I just want you to realize it is not about sex, it's a big part, but if I can be a part of your beautiful world, Colleen, for life, I'd be the happiest man ever. One day I am going to ask you to marry me! I hope it's not one of those issues where you need to think about it, but just say "yes" and make me the happiest man on the planet. My life revolves around disappointments, misleading's, and people who are users. I trust you with my kids, our kids, and my life! I love you, Colleen! My Queen. Yours and nobody else's P.W.

During some of their conversations, she told him about a couple of drive-by shootings in the area and how one day needed to move to a quieter place with less crime. The closer they got, he had thoughts of her being a part of their family in Clarksville.

He planted a seed in Colleen's mind about her moving down there. She did not seem to resist at all, she was ready to give real love a chance too. Even though he had moved his last two wives to Clarksville from other states, this time was completely different. They talked for July and decided that she needed to come down for a visit. They booked a flight and Colleen came down for a long weekend to meet PW in person and the children. He picked her up right after work and stared at her the whole time as she beamed with excitement.

They went for a drive, got a bite to eat, and got over the first-time meeting jitters quick. It felt like they had known each other for a long time, sort of old connected spirits. They went to the house to meet the children. They seemed open to her, though had been through so much with their mother and his second wife, they had some apprehension. That night, Colleen made everyone a spaghetti dinner and they had a good time, mixed with a little awkwardness. Afterward, PW took her to get some dairy-free ice cream and they hung out in the park downtown and talked for a long time. The next day, they spent the whole afternoon exploring downtown Clarksville and had lunch at a Bayou place. The entire day was spectacular. Her flight was the next day and they both knew they wanted to continue with their new bond and already started to miss one another.

When he drove her to the airport, he made lots of attempts to stall her getting on her flight, even a random stop at a Dairy Queen, for him to get some grub. She cried the entire time because she missed him and was stressed, she would miss her flight. Deep down, she was falling in love with him too, though she was much more guarded against her experience with dating in Chicago. The next couple of months were spent planning and talking a lot about their future. PW planned a road trip to Chicago for the family at the end of August. After a delay in getting a new battery for his truck and several hours later, they all arrived big-eyed in the city.

All of them were camped out on her condo floor and they went on many city adventures, including a pre-season NFL game between the Chicago Bears and Tennessee Titans. She made sure there was plenty of food around and the kids helped, her cook tacos and got hooked on Cheddar potato chips dipped in French Onion dip. They took the CTA downtown to take in the massive buildings and get some Chicago style deep dish and Stan's donuts. It was their first time in a major city and was a fantastic experience for them. The next couple of months were intense. She was about to uproot her life of 20 years in a major city and move to the South and move in with a new man, four children, two additional cats, and one dog.

PW had had enough of her living alone in an unsafe place and she had gotten used to living a life as a professional isolated hermit. PW gave her all his personal information and she took over the bills, formulated a plan for them, and took the bull by the horns. PW was so busy with work and being a single father, he had no one to put a structure and order into the home. They were also trying to decide the living arrangement. She hesitated and wanted to have a place of her own at first, however, he convinced her that it did not make sense to move twice. She agreed and made plans to live with them at Preston Drive. Her commitment was outstanding. She dove in to help him and the family out in more ways than anyone had ever done for him, including his two marriages.

They worked on bills together and on school packets for school. It was as if they had been partners for a long time. All the details of the move were buttoned up, including subletters for her condo and locking in professional movers. Things were moving so fast, yet everything was falling into place, which always means things are meant to be. There were some major barriers to get everything in order, yet they remained a solid team to work through any curve that was thrown their way. On the day of the move, the weather in Chicago had taken a dark turn. High winds and torrential rains had delayed PW's flight up there. She had to manage the movers themselves, load her car up by herself and catch her cats for the road trip to Tennessee. He was determined to get to Chicago as quickly as possible. His flight was supposed to land at 7 am, however due to delays arrived around 12:30 pm.

Colleen packed her car to the ceiling, with her cats in cages buried in her belongings, and headed out to pick him at Chicago O'Hare International airport. When she got out of the car, they hugged tightly for a long time and the tears from stress rolled down her cheeks. The joy she felt coupled with leaving a life of 20 years overwhelmed her. PW reassured her; he had her back always. He drove the entire way to Clarksville, taking the wheel like the real man that he is. The rest is history, the long wait for the one had become true, they were in love and taking life as it came to them, being there for each other as best friends and partners. With such a whirlwind past two months, they also had to adjust to their new life. She worked from home and started taking on some of the responsibilities of the home, such as grocery shopping, cooking, and laundry. They had gotten used to late dinners, messes, and digging through the laundry on the dining room table. Life is great and everyone was adjusting as best as they could to a new way of life. During this time, the

landlord continued to send hate texts to PW regarding the

agreement to stay, buy the house, or move out. Ultimately, they

decided to look for another place to live because the living

situation became uncertain. Initially, before Colleen had moved

down there, they tried to find a home to rent for the entire

family, including all of the pets. Hundreds of dollars later and

constant application denials they decided it would be a better

option to purchase a home. Shortly into the process of trying to

find a rental home, PW suggested the option of buying. One thing

about Colleen, is her intentions are from the heart, though she

can be hard-headed when ideas come from others. PW says all

that time living alone in a major city created an overly

independent woman who did not know how to rely on others. By

the grace of God, they found a fantastic real estate agent. They

spent many Saturday's looking at homes to buy, yet most of the

rooms in newer homes were small, which will not work for big

adult size children. Towards the end of their search, she decided to look at older, more sounds homes. What is meant to be will happen. The perfect size and the priced home was for sale, by a military family who got stationed in another city. They were eager to sell. In the first week of November 2019, they closed on their home. Finally, the uncertainty of a crazy landlord had ended, and they moved in the next day.

A few weeks later November 17, 2019, PW and Colleen became official and tied the knot at his boss's farm, by his wife, who is a minister. They got married on a goat farm in remote Tennessee, had delicious red velvet cake with sunflowers on it, and we're excited to continue their life together. After the ceremony, they went to Riverview Marina and had their wedding dinner. As PW says often, "I love my life" He finally had everything he wanted and importantly, he found and married the love of his life, a true queen, ride or die woman he had longed for since a young man.

CHAPTER 7 GENDER INEQUALITY AND RACISM

From the heart and soul of PW regarding discrimination, he is serious and clear about black men, including his own experiences in life and within family law. In his own words, "Black men are discriminated by other black men, white men, white females and at times black women." He stated it all stems back to Jim Crow and slavery and the lies made up about black men. After slavery was abolished, black men got jobs doing their best to become successful in a world that hates back men. Black men are viewed as animals and have every card stacked against them in life, even within their race, yet must press on through the gut-wrenching decades of pain to make great lives for themselves.

There are two types of black men our culture sees: worthless that will not succeed, or their determination and survival skills are going to prove everyone wrong. He said most other men may take a bullet when the cards are stacked so high against you, yet a black man will keep fighting and pushing on with every ounce of his energy. He posed a question though,

"Should the black man keep fighting and for how long, since the cards have not changed much for equality and the perception which is portrayed by society. When they march, they are "aggressive" When they take a knee they are "unamerican" It seems as if every move they make, society deems them aggressive. If a black man becomes successful within a dominant prestigious while male industry, he is seen as a "token" black man and a sell-out by some of his people. Even though he knows there are kind strong black women holding it down, with his experience with black women, they became defense and judgmental too. Often, he heard, "Where are all the good black men who are successful in holding down a good job and being great fathers to their children?" None of them ever saw the obvious or questions in a discriminatory society, why a single black father, who is a "piece of shit" has full custody of his four children he had with one woman, with whom he stayed married and faithful to for over 13 years. He often went without meals, so his kids could have full belly's. He went without clean clothes, so his children could go to school looking well put together. Is he still deadbeat in your eyes?

Depending on how wide you choose your lenses to be, there is significant racial and gender bias woven into a web of bureaucracy for single black fathers facing custody battles with the non-custodial parent. When most people think about child custody, they immediately think about single mothers who are struggling. This is a fair assumption because many children in custody cases are awarded to the mother. Why though? The big picture reason is that they are the mother, and mothers are deemed more nurturing than fathers. Yes, it is natural for children to run to a mother for a band-aid, snack, or to talk about what is bothering them. Does this make the father void of not making a safe place for his children to land because of his gender?

As stated in an article by Christina Vanvuran from May of 2017, "According to the 2013 United States Census, 13.4 million parents are deemed "custodial" and, of those, 1 in every 6

(17.5%) are fathers. That means about 2.5 million households are run by single fathers, many of which have a non-custodial counterpart. This, according to the Pew Research Center, is up from 300,000 in 1960." The trend of single father households is growing, which means that being a non-custodial mother is, too.

According to the National Parent's Association, men have a greater tendency to be gainfully employed to contribute to the needs of the family. 73.4% of custodial fathers worked full-time year-round, while only 50.1% of custodial mothers did. Custodial mothers were due, on average, $5,176 per year from non-custodial fathers, who paid $3,579 for 69.1%. By contrast, custodial fathers were due only $4,471 per year and received only $2,797 for 62.6%. NC mothers, although they had substantially lower child support obligations, still paid a lower percentage. Why is there such a disparity between what is ordered by the courts and a significant deficit of child support enforcement between males and females?

According to a Census Bureau report of 2005 statistics, paying to support their children is something non-custodial mothers are not great at. In PW's case, the mother knows how to play the system extremely well, knowing because of her gender she can make a $25 one-time payment, and the child support views this effort to pay and makes no attempt to enforce the court-ordered amount, even though the back child support is behind $20,000.

Meanwhile, PW works long hours at an ok paying job, donates plasma, shops at Dollar Tree to keep his family safe and secure. He told a story about a Chiropractor he knew who came from a poor family, worked his way through college, and built up his practice, and was doing well. He got married to whom he thought was the love of his life, had two children, and was living a fantastic life. The wife did not work, took care of the children, and cheated on him several times. The court awarded the mother the children and she raked him over the coals for child support and was granted an increase from $2,500-$3,500 per month. Where is the accountability of how the money is justified and being spent by these con artist goal diggers? He was forced to live in a small apartment, lost his business, and was sent to jail for being $1,000 behind. Every year his practice was audited to see if his profits increased. If so, she received more child support. This is a robbery. In a recent conversation on a job site with a Nashville police officer, PW was not surprised at the officer's custody battle challenges. He was white, a tenured officer with a clean track record, and also had custody of his kids. The mother was a drug addict, got clean in three months, and started her games to see how much she can get out of him. He is a police officer! What makes a decent hard-working father any more than an ATM in these types of women's minds? They know exactly what they are doing. Did we forget she chose to cheat and abandon her children? Why isn't more light shined on the demographic of deadbeat moms? It is as if people choose to turn a blind eye and wonder how a mother can be this way. They do a poorer job of it than do Non-custodial fathers, even though their child support burden is less onerous than men's. The report

shows 13.6 million parents with custody of 23 million children

who had another parent living elsewhere. Physical custody was

given to 84% female and 16% male. About 7.8 million of those

parents had some form of a child support order in effect, but

mothers were far more likely than fathers to be the beneficiaries

of support orders.

Almost 61.4% of custodial mothers had support orders in

effect. This number was only around 36.4% of custodial fathers.

That means there were about 800,000 custodial dads with child

support orders and a little over 7 million custodial moms with

orders. PW told another story about a man who raised his two

children to the age of 15 by himself because the mother had a

long history of heroin abuse. They were thriving as a family; the

kids were involved in school activities and their grades were

fantastic. This case seems cut and dry, however, the mom got

clean for three months and the courts ripped his children from

his home to give the mom a chance. He became so depressed

and destroyed that he attempted suicide. He went to trauma counseling, remarried to a wonderful woman, and was able to see his kids. Soon after her children were living with her, the mother used heroin again, overdosed and they placed the kids back into his custody. Was the decision in this case worth the pain of what the family endured? People deserve second chances; however, a hasty decision was made by the courts because she was the mother, and she did not have enough time to stay clean. A gradual process would have been a better decision.

At the core of these situations, the children suffer the most, emotionally, and financially. PW knows there are other father's out there doing their best to do what is best for the families. The even smaller piece of the pie is race and the color of PW's skin. He is automatically judged by the internal bias of lawyers, child support offices, and judges. For over 400 years black men have been labeled animals, incarcerated in much higher numbers, and labeled deadbeats dads. Today's culture does not paint a positive picture of black men either. They are socially brutalized, through images from the media and labeled violent. Reality shows make it acceptable to glamorize black men being a baby daddy to multiple children with multiple women. PW does not deny the fact that there are plenty of deadbeat parents out there, mothers and fathers. He is the father of all four children, the same mother and he stayed married to her during a time where most people would have cheated and left the family. With the divorce rates being so high, he is an anomaly.

An article from the Huffington Post from February 2014 states that the scornful term deadbeat dad has become popular in describing fathers who do not uphold their legal reasonability. Most of the fathers under this label love their children and 66% of them are not able to afford the child support and continue to get painted with a broad brush. What about "deadbeat" moms who can pay yet choose to not contribute to their family's' best interest. One cannot blame them, because they are not scared into doing what is right and the child support office turns a blind eye because they are a female. Iyeisha Nycole Miller's research project from 2014, called African American Fathers: Life as a Single Parent, states for decades now, non-custodial parents, mainly non-custodial fathers, have been fighting for their rights to be an active presence in their children's lives. They feel strongly that they should be able to do so without the interference of the courts and the custodial parent. However, the various social systems already set in place (i.e. schools, courts, etc.) often disregard these parents' roles in their children's lives.

As if the battle for equality is not enough to endure with society, courts, and child support offices, social services may come to investigate the home to make sure the proper living environment is set up for the children. When PW got the family out of the homeless shelter, he had to buy new furniture and stock the refrigerator at all times. Why? If one of the children calls their mother and complains that they are hungry, she can call child services on him to investigate. Typically, the children are complaining about not having endless boxes of fruit roll-ups,

when he makes sure they have meat, cheese, milk, and cereal.

When he has a spontaneous visit from social services and

everything checks out fine, it remains a negative mark on his

record. Keep in mind they have lost everything because of their

mother's actions which include furniture, toys, and baby pictures

from the eviction from their apartment and storage unit.

According to the guidelines of social services, adequate

furniture is needed, which forced him to choose high-interest

weekly payment plans to purchase what was needed. She had

also ruined his credit score and with no money, he had no other

option to choose. Single father's especially black fathers are

constantly under the microscope. PW stated when he takes the

family on road trip vacations, he always keeps a copy of the

parenting plan with him, because if he gets pulled over the

officer will question if he is the custodial parent. If the mother

decides to not show up on a date, she agreed upon to drop off

the children, he must file a kidnapping report with the police, and he will get investigated for the incident. PW has experienced heavy bias in the courtroom. Before she ran off to be with another man and move to Missouri, she did not show up in Tennessee for the Child Support court-ordered date.

At this point, she was $10,000 behind and the Missouri child support office was not enforcing the case and giving her preferential treatment because she is a white female. The judge asked "Is Miss Davis here? He immediately asks PW, "I see your $10,000 behind" I need to lock you up right away!" PW said back "Hold up, I am the custodial parent" The judge gave a puzzled look and gave the defendant 2 hours to show up. Then he asks PW where she is and he says, "I do know sir, she was ordered to be here." The judge lashed out and said, "Don't tell me how to run my courtroom!" Feeling frustrated, he asked the judge "Your honor, I lost a day pay and I am struggling to put food on the table for my four children." His response was "It is not my problem." Are you awake and outraged by racial and gender inequality?

An overview of our prison system ties back to only one thing, the color of one's skin. According to the Urban Institute in an article called "A Matter of Time, black people are incarcerated five times that of white people. When Monica, an African American woman was serving her 28 years in prison, there were 400 women at the prison and three white females at the facility at that time. If laws are in place, how come many white females' escape being brought to justice? In the Marshall Project by Michelle Hadley, she describes one story of many of how privileged white women's lives are saved by the color of their skin. Rachel, age 70, an African American woman was in prison for allegedly kidnapping her teen children out of an orphanage. This act is nearly impossible without their consent, however, a white female social worker agreed to help her.

Since Rachel did not fall in line with the social worker, she called the cops on her, when she had not even made a move to get her children out. Fate had landed Rachel and Michelle who is white in the same cell together. Michelle Hadley, a white woman was falsely arrested for a case where Angela Diaz plotted a scheme to create fake accounts, making it appear she was a violent stalker and kidnapper. Hadley spent three months in jail before prosecutors determined that she was an innocent victim, and was fully cleared of any wrongdoing. Though her time was only three months, African Americans face much stiffer jail sentences. The systemic racism goes so deep, that all of the deputies told Michelle, "You do not look like you belong here" It was clear to Michelle she would be treated with respect and dignity, much different from her elderly cellmate, Rachel. Michelle knew she could help her cellmate obtain basic needs, such as clean clothes and food. She chose to use her white privilege to help an innocent woman out, who was targeted by all the deputies. How does this tie into child support laws and family law for a single black father? It has everything to do with race and gender inequality.

Even though the number of white females going to prison has increased according to the Washington Post, that is mainly due to the population of white females increasing over the past decades. The numerous incidents and data have been highlighted to show how bias and asleep society is when it comes to single black fathers doing what is best for their families. How can a mother lose custody of her children? In these types of cases, the mother is hyper-focused on the father, herself, and not the children. The mother choosing to not accept to listen to feedback from others including the courts to make personal improvements. Extreme examples of what some women do to exaggerate are ludicrous. For instance, if a child has trouble going to the bathroom, a crazy mom focused on the father can tell others, including caseworkers that he is molesting their child. That statement somehow gets into the minds of others, including the judge and it poses a threat to a father getting custody of the children from an unfit mother.

There are cases where mothers have demanded their children to accuse their father of sexual abuse and if they do not follow orders, they will leave them. In PW's situation, one of the tactics the mother used to convince the children that their dad was giving her daily beatings was going into another room and close the door during a verbal argument and yell, "Don't beat me again."

Lastly, in the case of an African American man named Jerimiah Sampson, his three-year custody battle finally awarded him full custody of a son whom he never knew he had. He received an out-of-the-blue phone call from an adoption agency claiming that he may be the father of his son. He said, no adoption here, I am the father. He jumped through hoops to get in contact with the mother. While he was in constant contact with the mother, she went silent. When he got to her place, the door got slammed in his face and the neighbor said the boy got adopted three weeks ago. He was devastated and hired a lawyer to get his son back on what money he had. Amid all the struggle, the girlfriend suddenly wanted to be a part of their lives, even though it had been a tremendous amount of time and initially she received visitation.

Typically, the motive is to get the court system on her side because she may gain the financial support of some sort. After several trips back and forth to Florida which was a five-hour drive, in July 2011 the judge annulled the adoption, and around Christmas time, was awarded full custody of his son. Through these prior examples, one can see how biased society, the court system, and child support offices are when it comes to fathers having rights to their children and gaining custody of their children, especially when the mother is unfit. Yes, it is possible for females to not be healthy for their children. Even though the demographic is not large enough for society to pay attention to, the issues barrel down to two specific issues, discrimination based on gender and skin color. PW knows exactly who is, a man of integrity who loves his family, and knows the challenges he faces every day as a single black father.

CHAPTER 8 CHILD SUPPORT HANDBOOKS VS REALITY

One would think once the divorce decree is finalized, the parties agree, and all documents are signed that the law will be upheld? This is not the case for single black fathers or fathers in general. In a prior chapter, the amount of evidence PW had to gather took years to gather and the evidence had to prove abandonment of the children on several occasions. The physical file is too large to fit in a normal size hanging folder and contains every piece of critical evidence for him to be awarded custody of his four children. What is messed up is that the mother can put on her best Hollywood cry scene, make assumptions, file false police reports, lie and the world believes her sob story as if she were a woman of the cloth. When the court takes a recess, on the outside of the court, she is laughing to friends and vindictively says, "I am going to get this nigger."

From the beginning of the order in May of 2017, the pattern continues of working the system well. She has a long, yet hard to prove con artist ways to mooch off the system in other ways. The role she chooses to play is manipulative, immoral, and geared at getting back at the father when she is destroying her children's self-worth and lives. Our culture views the father as the provider and the woman as the nurturer and often have a puzzled look and have a hard time believing mothers are capable of any wrongdoing. How does all this work? It does not work well for single black fathers. The number one issue single fathers face is the mother's not paying their court-ordered child support. Ever since the final divorce decree and parenting plan was ordered, the mother has been playing the system to her benefit. She is required to pay around $871 per month for four children, which is much less than most fathers will pay because the courts determine a man's income potential is much higher than a woman.

The failure of the non-custodial parent to support a minor child who is legally obligated to pay and has the means to do so is a crime in the state of Missouri. This is a felony offense if a parent does not pay for 6 months at a time within 12 months. Also. If the parent has accumulated an excess of $5,000 there is potential may be charged as a felony. In PW's situation, the amount of back child support owed is around $20,000 and during the past 4 years, the mother will pay occasionally, even if it is $25 to confuse the child support office into thinking she is paying consistently. From August 2019 through April 2020 not a dime was paid to support her four children that she lost custody of through her actions. PW would be sent to jail after 30 days without paying. The mother is supposed to let the child support office know her current address and employer yet chooses not to. PW has had the child support offices ask him where she is working because she makes it a priority to stay off the radar.

The parenting plan requires the mother to visit the children every third Thursday of the month. She is required to notify the primary parent via text message, Thursday before 4 pm that she will be able to make her visitation. This never happens. She chooses to create a vicious cycle of telling the kids when she may or may not visit often leading to confusion and broken promises. She has failed to make her court-ordered visitation and every time visitation is set up, the terms are in her favor and she sometimes drops the kids off early with no notice or changes the time the morning of to suit her needs. Either way, she is not building a relationship with her children by spending more time with them. May I reiterate, she chose to move away to Missouri from the children to chase a relationship with a man whom she gave money to from the bank accounts she drained on the way out. The relationship was brief, the mystery man took the money and cut his ties. The mother has been in civil contempt of court for a long time, yet PW is busy working late hours to provide for his family, there is no time or financial means to hire a lawyer to get her to pay her obligation.

Other tactics used by the Child Support Office include taking away one's driver's license to get them to pay or threaten to take their passport. PW stated that the mother was still running on a Tennessee driver's license even though she has been living in Missouri for years. These rules are clearly stated in

the Missouri and Tennessee Child Support Handbooks, however,

when it comes to single black fathers, they turn a blinds eye and

give favoritism to the mothers. PW clearly stated a child support

employee from the Missouri child support office said, "We favor

women, and single fathers are a low priority."

It is mind-boggling why any child support office does not

prosecute and collect as much child support as possible since

they receive a portion of the payments. He has been given the

run around by both the Tennessee and Missouri child support

offices. He has made close to 60 phone calls to each office this

past year. When he calls, the hold times are significant and are

constantly been told a letter out on a specific date and we need

to give the non-custodial more time. Why? Because she is a white

female, who happens to be a mother. The amount of red tape he

must go through to receive any support is astronomical. When he

spoke to the Missouri office recently, he was told the case was

submitted to the district attorney for family law. He called the district attorney's office and they stated they are not able to even begin to register this case with the court, simply because the non-custodial party has not responded. She was given a response date of July 9th, it is now August 17.

In a recent conversation with the local Montgomery County Child Support Office, PW had a solid conversation with his new caseworker. She stated their hands are tied when the non-custodial parent is living under the radar and does not comply and gave him the advice to retain a lawyer. They can send our multiple letters, attempt to find out where they work, and if the other parent is not responding, they have limited authority to go further. Additionally, they are bombarded with cases backed up for years. He appreciated her honesty when he was told, they have four addresses on file for the non-custodial party and they only have the authority to do so much.

Why are mothers above the law and how do they receive so much leniency? From a cultural and historical perspective, women have been considered superior because their children may not survive without their mothers, since men are not able to nurse and men cannot breastfeed babies. What if the biological mother is not nurturing, is involved in drugs, lays around all day doing nothing, cheats on her husband, and chooses to nurse a liquor bottle? As a society, are we that ignorant about the possibility of women being unfit mothers? How far must the damage of unfit mothers be before our culture becomes awake and realizes this is a matter of what is wrong versus right. Ultimately the children suffer and develop unhealthy coping skills at a young age they will carry into their adult lives. Women get special treatment because they are a woman, especially white females, though they are not reported in the media.

CHAPTER 9 PSYCHOLOGY OF ABANDONED CHILDREN

PW's wife once said I would rather take a punch to the face than to be the victim of all forms of verbal abuse. According to the Center for Disease Control, an estimated 56 percent of all abusers, physical, mental, and sexual -- are women. The most common form is psychological. Verbal abusive manifests in many forms, such as name-calling, threatening abandonment, body harm, scapegoating, or blame, using sarcasm, berating the other parent. One of the sneakiest forms of abuse is gaslighting which is a type of abuse that distorts one's perception of reality and questions every memory they have. Children are supposed to look up to adults for wisdom and their minds are sponges absorbing overnight in their environments.

When a mother implants tiny seeds for years, the children are at high risk for issues in life and as adults. In case of the abuse coming from the mother, the children end up protecting her, even when part of their mind they know it feels wrong. Why? Colleen nicknamed it umbilical cord syndrome, which is not a scientific term, yet a name for an attempt to explain the bond a birth mother has during the womb and through giving birth. A Dana.org article titled, "The Fear in Love," explains, "The neurotransmitter is released in massive amounts at birth and during bonding with the mother. It is also released when they are in pain. This dual role for norepinephrine sets us on the path to explore the fundamental, and puzzling, the question of why a child cannot learn to break the attachment to an abusive caregiver. After all, when humans and all other mammals experience pain, they learn to avoid anything that warns of the pain so that they can prevent it next time. In an abusive relationship, why doesn't the pain activate the brain's fear and avoidance circuits?

Possibly, the area of the brain responsible for fear and avoidance is not turned on by children not old enough to leave the nest, which in turn has the chance of altering our genes. Think of our genes as a library of information. How we are treated by parents lays the foundation of who children become and reside in a great part of early childhood experiences. Epigenetic changes also occur in abusive situations and what is challenging with verbal abuse, is the reinforcement of negative information over years creates welded highways in the subconscious mind. What is detrimental to brain development is when neglect or abuse produces a heightened or prolonged activation of the stress system results in later life difficulty.

What does verbal abuse look like? The following are examples of behavior as a result of verbal abuse. Children may seem unconfident or lack self-assurance, struggle to control their emotions, have difficulty making or maintaining relationships act and in a way that is inappropriate for their age. As they get older they may use the language you wouldn't expect them to know for their age, act in a way or know about things you wouldn't expect them to know for their age, struggle to control their emotions, have extreme outbursts, seem isolated from their parents lack social skills and have few or no friends.

How is the behavior of PW's children affected by the actions of their mother? Deep down the children are four individual gifts from God and what is explained is behavior that has been brain mapped at an early age. They are too young to understand the coping mechanism they adapted to out of survival of their home that was breaking apart. Children do not have a choice of what circumstances they are brought into. When they become adults and are out of the nest, they will start to understand how critical the environment is to shape their perception of the world.

The oldest and only girl is the artist and brings anime characters to life and particularity their clothing. She has a radiant smile and has fantastic dancing skills. At times she and her youngest brother figure out routines and post them on TikTok. At a young age, PW said she wanted to become a pediatrician. She was also involved in cheerleading and was phenomenal. As time has gone on, her desires and dreams started to decline and she started having trouble believing in herself.

A behavior she learned from her mother is manipulation. On several occasions, she manipulates her brothers into doing things for her. One time she convinced one of her brothers to give up his Pepsi and Taki's for a ½ a slice of cheesecake. He blindly got tricked and she walked away smiling saying "give them a little and you can get a lot" PW"s wife nipped that in the butt real quick and told her, "What you did was wrong, not fair, and that behavior will hurt you one day." She is not a bad person. Her heart is big, though she has learned how to act this way from her mother.

The oldest son, JC is kindhearted, flighty, and has a huge smile. He has a heightened sense of responsibility and does his best to keep his brothers and sister on time and responsible. Underneath, he is challenged with worrying and getting stressed over certain things. PW's wife helps him with moments where he experiences anxiety, though does not let him use his feelings as a crutch either. Cornbread is challenged with impulse control and is always fighting with people, which he learned from his mother. He is told to walk away when he gets pestered by a school kid, though when pushed too far, he chooses to be physical.

Cornbread stays in his world, keeps his walls up, and thank God for his love of fishing and the outdoors. When he is fishing, he is smiling. He stays in his mind, cooks well, loves to try new foods with his family, such as Indian food. He is the only kid that loves to eat seafood. When we treated him to a seafood dinner for his birthday he was in heaven. He is sort of our house "brah" kid and is physically strong for his age. He gets into scuffles with his older brother over silly kid stuff and it is like watching Godzilla and King Kong having an epic battle.

It is best to be non-reactive when he is engaged in behavior where he trying to get a rise out of someone. When he feels attacked, he goes right into defensive fight mode. When he is being reprimanded or yelled at, he completely shuts down. He has opened up to PW's wife more over this past year and her ability to connect with people creates a space where she is not a threat to him, yet more of a consultant. He also knows she means business. His relationship with his mother is turbulent. He has had the most difficult time because of his age when she left.

After the winter break visit, he came back with deep scratches on his forearms. When PW asked him and the kids about it, they covered for their mom and vaguely said there was an altercation. This past June, there was another situation with the cousins from their sister's kids. Cornbread said a kid threw ice down his back and he told the kid to stop. The kid did not stop, so Cornbread punched the cousin and said he was a brat. In elementary school, he has had incidents on the bus and altercations with teachers. He is a great kid underneath all the layers of verbal abuse from his mother and only knows how to solve most situations with violence.

Lastly, the youngest, KK the home's dance talent and will be a famous actor one day. He is a social butterfly and whenever he hears great beats to a song, he has to get his body dancing. He is obsessed with winning on fortnight against his gaming buddies. We often hear high pitched screams when he is playing an intense game. He has struggled with throwing tantrums to get what he wants. If he sees one of his siblings getting a tab bit of attention, he has a hard time controlling his need to barge in and become noticed. PW admits, that both he and his mother gave in when he had tantrums, which is partly to blame for his behavior. He is doing his best to adapt to his newer stepmom and has nicknamed her Kool-Aid Miracle Whip and we have no idea why.

The purpose of these stories is to shed light on how powerful the mother has influenced her children's behavior in various forms. Princess has learned the same manipulation skills her mother uses to get what she wants, even though it hurts the ones you are supposed to love. Because of the mother's unhealthy behavior, the boys have an undertone of fear of abandonment. In their developing minds, if they do not follow what she says, they will be left behind by their mother. This is also true when they interact with their sister too, they have this slight sense of fear of her. There is a high possibility she may get used by her mother, like generations of unhealthy behavior patterns abuse in the family.

PW admitted that he has always treated her like a princess with nice birthdays and especially on Valentine's Day. He also tells her she is smart and beautiful. Their relationship is somewhat distant now and I know his heart hurts some because she is not daddy's little girl anymore. He will always love her and knows she will have to fall on her face in life because of what has been ingrained in her mind. PW feels his oldest son is starting to figure small things about his mother and has a "whatever" attitude about it.

JC did mention that his mom goes overboard in public fighting for certain things and he walks away to disassociate himself with the situation. The youngest, KK is the one the mother manipulates the most and spoils. He throws the most tantrums in her presence and raises the most stink in the home especially after being around his mother. She caves every time and does not know he is being set up for failure in the real world. When one is giving attention to the other siblings, he butts in and starts to dance to get attention or break up the conversations. You can feel his energy and urgency to be seen when his siblings are getting more attention, almost as if it will kill him inside if he does not get the instant gratification his mind is telling him to get. The parenting solution is to continue to love the children unconditionally, support them in their journeys, guide them, and teach them how to be solid members of society. The path they are on is not linear, it is and will continue to be full of ups and downs, yet with strong faith, patience and love, we pray they will be able to overcome their circumstances and lead productive lives full of gratitude and passion.

CHAPTER 10 FAMILY INCIDENTS AUG 2019- CURRENT

8/27/19

PW received a call from the school around 11:31 am to report

that their mother had attempted to meet the kids at their

schools, which are in the same area as each other to have lunch

with them. In her usual fashion, she showed up unannounced.

Her text messages to PW that day were demanding. She said she

was in town for court and said he is preventing her from seeing

her children and made it out to seem he was keeping them from

her. She went to Kenwood High School first, Kenwood Middle

School second and lastly, Kenwood Elementary school. The

mother manipulated her way into the elementary school and had

lunch with the youngest, KK in the school cafeteria.

Unfortunately, KK being so young only saw his mommy in front of

him and no idea of what she had done. It is against the child

parenting agreement to show up without prior notice. The other

messed up part is that the elementary school alerted PW, not the high school or middle school. When packets are filled out each year that the district distributes, there are specific areas of who is designated to pick them up or meet them at school. Due to her violent and unstable history, the mother is not listed on the packet, nor is her driver's license scanned in their system. These rules are supposed to protect the children, yet again gender bias in favor of the mother creates an unsafe soft spot in people's hearts, of "but she's the mother" Is she though? This is a woman who showed up in the middle of the night with some random man and a gun at their home on Preston drive. PW was livid when he received the call from the elementary school and asked them how she was able to even get into the school and they knew they were wrong, yet proceeded to dance in circles to attempt to cover their ass. PW asked for an incident report from all three schools and never received one.

8/27/20

PW asked KK, age 9 at the time if his mom came to see him, he said, yes, they had lunch in the school cafeteria. He said that she could not check him out to have lunch because his dad would not let him and she showed him the entire text message conversation, which was an adult conversation, which breaks the rules of the parenting plan. This is an example of gaslighting, a known tactic of manipulators that alters one's sense of reality. The subtle and slick verbal abuse is what she does constantly to paint a horrific picture of their father where they resent him. A child's mind is not developed enough to question the fake reality that is established, however they are old enough as early as the age of 4 to absorb unhealthy behavior patterns such as manipulation, which he uses and learned from this mother. PW also asked what else did your mom say to you and he said that his mommy told him that daddy was taking the child support money and blowing it on football games and Colleen, his girlfriend at the time. The fact is, there have been no child support payments since the end of July and nonpayment continues for nine consecutive months. Also, this supposed money blowing includes taking the kids to football games too.

8/31/19

The obsession continues from their mother and Facebook friend

request notification came from PW's only daughter came to

Colleen. PW asked Princess about it said she did not send a

request. The notification disappeared. This behavior is not

uncommon for the mother. PW's second wife was harassed by

his first wife via text, Facebook, and phone calls and created

tension for the family. The mother will play nice and do her best

to weave her way into your mind and pretend to be your friend

to conquer and cause problems within the family. PW knows she

has resentment towards him, however, her actions and

documented incidents of partying, violence, and abandonment of

the children led to the courts having PW be the resident parent.

This is almost unheard of an according to an article by Samara

Lynn from June 2019, her father is part of a 4% slice of the

demographic and still the most ignored or unknown group. In her

article, she states "My father had little to no resources,

sometimes worked multiple jobs with over a two-hour commute

to stay afloat and keep the lights on. Think about this. If the roles were reversed the father would be in jail immediately, his child support stacking up and when he got out, will be reprimanded by the court system to work three jobs. Seem fair?

9/16/19

Colleen was doing homework with KK at the dining room table and being educated herself understands the importance of dedication and education. Cornbread called for KK to call their mom back. He had been on the phone with their mom and she was asking for his younger brother. On some level, she loves her children, though from the outside in, her love is toxic and conditional. The other reason she talks to the youngest is that he is the most vulnerable to manipulate and get information from and especially tells him to make our lives a living hell by his actions. I asked him to finish his homework before he called his mom back, so he could be free for the rest of the night. KK was positive after school and was excited about his room that I arranged and thanked me for it. After the phone call ended with his mom, his behavior got hyper, he started climbing all over the dresser and table and ignored his father and Colleen. Then video calls came in around 5:10 pm which added more fuel to the fire. As parents, we spend time having to de-escalate the results of a phone conversation with their mother.

9/25/20

Since she does not send court-ordered child support, he decided to call upon Colleen's paperwork skills and start sending certified letters along with an itemized bill for 50% of the food costs. He had no other choice to act because affording a lawyer is not possible. Lord knows if you have four kids and three of them are growing boys, they eat everything in sight, drink gallons of milk and still stare into the refrigerator 15 minutes after dinner. Additionally, significant more evidence is needed in court if you are male to have them even consider enforcing child support because she is a woman, however, she can lie, cry and pretend to play the role of victim with false police reports and the courts will be in her favor. He also sent a letter certified mail to attempt to collect 60% of Princess's orthodontist bill to the only known address in Missouri. Again, she is supposed to let the child support office in Missouri know her current address and chooses not to. This living situation is unhealthy, multi families live in a duplex, the youngest of the sisters was in prison and when the kids visit their mom, they sleep all cramped up in their mom's room.

10/7/19

A video call to KK came in around 8 pm. Colleen happened to walk by to the laundry room to switch out the load and heard her say "I can't wait to see my baby, my baby" This is an example of a baby talking to the youngest. It gives them the temporary satisfaction of feeling loved by their mother. PW and their mother split up when he was young, which is the foundation for his up and down emotions especially from talking to his mother.

10/8/19

KK was in the car with Colleen headed to a Math Class event at his school and he said that his mom told him, she was done with her classes and is now a nurse. She used to help elderly people. PW has no idea where she works, neither does the child support office. She is supposed to let them know where she works, to keep up with the payments, and has not done so.

10/9/19

The endless phone calls to the Tennessee and Missouri child support office make this situation even muddier. There are long hold times, huge employee turnover, and more importantly, PW getting the run-around. For over two years he has been calling both offices and continues to receive answers such as "we sent a letter, she has 30 days to respond" or we never received paperwork to proceed. We all know that the child support office is a complete bureaucracy. Since they receive a portion of the payment, one would think that would motivate them to proceed with the fullest extent of the child support handbook and enforce the cases?

Patrick Davis called the Child Support Office in TN, they gave him a balanced owed of $12,875.51 owed, and per his request had the call transferred to his current caseworker where he left VM 9:34 a.m.) to get a status of a payment that is 60 days past due.

10/9/19

9:48 am Patrick Davis spoke with Missouri Child Support Office. Spoke with a customer service representative and they said a request had been made from TN Child Support Office to their office on 9/18/19 regarding past-due child support.

10/11/19

She is supposed to let PW know if her plans to pick up the children for a visit, instead she confuses and tells the children all sorts of visit dates. He works 2 hours away from home and needs significant lead time to plan for visitation. Children need to live stress-free lives and they do not need the games and responsibility placed upon their shoulders. They are kids and they get sidetracked and forget what has been told to them, then when PW doesn't cater to her schedule, which is often the last minute, she proceeds to tell the world he is late or not letting her see the children. The text below is from 10/10/19, only two days before. The meeting spot is at the designated Walmart spot on Wilma Rudolph Road. One important piece of advice PW gave Colleen was during a drop-off, especially if you are by yourself, do not say anything to her, and keep your distance. She has filed false police reports on me and if you say one thing, she will tell the police you assaulted her and get the children to lie for her.

10/20/20

The mother dropped the kids off at Walmart at 1:17 pm All of the kids appeared to have a good time. Cornbread and KK got haircuts and JC said when the mother took them to get haircuts, she told the stylist that we never get them haircuts. KK had a new silver necklace, a Star Wars movie, and Cornbread said he was given lots of money for a fish tank. Everyone seemed back to normal. Around 3:30 pm KK was in tears and said he had a headache. Colleen gave him kids liquid Tylenol. Princess started him a bath. He laid down in his bed afterward. KK came to Colleen around 3:45 pm and said "I have something really important to tell you. "They went to his room to talk in private. He said, "I do not you to feel bad when I tell you this, but I want to live with my mommy" He then burst into tears and said he misses her and we talked about how that must feel. He said he did not want to tell anyone else. I asked PW to come to talk with us together and we found out that in the car that she asked KK to help her financially. He said he wanted to go live with his mom. PW told him he cannot live with his mom, because there is no room there, since she lives with her mom, sister, sister's boyfriend. Also, PW told him you are a child, be a kid, you do not need the weight of her troubles on your shoulders. He also said that we are not trying to tell you not to love your mom, she loves you and you love her, and if she says things that make you feel bad you need to tell her that makes you feel bad and I am a kid.

PW talked about when they tried to offer her to Clarksville, TN. In May 2019, PW offered to give back 50% of the child support money for 6 months to get closer to her children. KK relayed the information to her, and she told her she met someone and did not want to leave a new relationship that would be mean to someone new and walk out of their life like that. She said he would not take the offer is because she was not paying child support. KK did say she is working full-time, which we have no evidence of. We both said we loved him very much and to be a leader, be his person, and to be a kid. We encouraged him to talk to us to get things off your chest. PW also explained what it means to try and control someone and what it means to be a leader and that he was proud of him for wanting to help his blood family out. We also explained that you are not able to make someone make any choices and you must be careful to not help someone who does not help themselves. Colleen made him a grilled cheese and he fell asleep from his tears of confusion and exhaustion. She posts pictures of the children at the beginning of the visit intentionally. She wants the world to believe that she is an incredible mother. There have been times where she will buy clothes for the photography session and then take the clothes back or tell the children to leave them in Missouri with her, which is a form of control.

10/20/19

Text messages sent to KK are for adult ears only. Kids need to be kids and not feel responsible to help their mother. He is so vulnerable and has developed a false sense of self, pleading with his mom to move to an apartment near him. She chose to move to Missouri and follow a new relationship, instead of being close to her children and dared to tell her kids that it is not fair to a new relationship to not give it attention. What about your babies, the angels you carried for 9 months? He was begging her to move back and she always states how she is working on getting her financial situation figured out which makes him feel helpless that he has no means to help save her.

10/22/19

Colleen received a Facebook request from KK Davis. I asked him if he sent me a Facebook request and he said no. This was an attempt for their mother to contact Colleen and begin her pattern of attempting to befriend her. My current wife is a strong-willed and emotionally intelligent woman. Her confidence level is high, and it is beneath her to get hooked into the negative that is being started.

10/23/19

KK pretended to be sick today so he can get out of school. I said I can give you some gum for your tummy, mint helps with that. He said, it never works, stormed off, slammed doors, ignored me. He did get ready for school. Overall, their attitudes are disrespectful at times which is the result of manipulation from the birth mom. Princess is snappy at her dad and ignores him and JC threw a fit at Colleen when she wanted to put KK's chicken patty on the same cookie sheet for dinner one night. Most of their behavior stems from the manipulation and the mother telling the children how much of a worthless father he is. They are too young to understand to know that their mother is manipulating them, yet they know exactly what they are doing when they try to get the things they want. We started having difficulties with Cornbread's impulsive behavior and anger. Deep down he is a great kid, loves fishing and the outdoors. He hates school and is always on the offensive when anyone confronts him a little or bumps him at school. This behavior is directly influenced by the abandonment of his mother, their dysfunctional relationship, and her personality which is dramatic in public and in conversations that she has with others. This type of behavior is combative, lacks understanding, and damages the children's ability to manage their emotions. Below is one of many examples of phone calls, e-mails, and meetings with teachers and school staff.

Unfortunately, as much as you explain the situation, there are no resources to help with behavior modification and you often get the blank stare and head tilt as if they understand, however, they do not, unless they have walked a mile in PW's shoes. Colleen, his girlfriend has been a huge support for a while. She was naively excited about her first teacher conference with KK and PW in the fall. The entire time, the teacher had a conversation with Colleen and not PW. Colleen knew the teacher had deep-rooted biases towards black men. PW has always been involved with meetings, homework, and school play even though every time he walks in a room, he will be looked at like he is the rare white buffalo in Janesville, WI. He does not pay attention to the energy and keeps fighting for what is right.

10/24/19

Thu, Oct 24, 2:47 PM (5 days ago)

to me

Mr. Davis,

I placed a major referral for Cornbread's behavior today. Coming back from lunch, I expect my students to be in a quiet and single-file line. Cornbread's, and a few other students, were not meeting this expectation. I went over to where they were in line and reminded them of the expectation. Cornbread responded by saying, "why are you talking to me? I'm not the only one!"

He is correct that he was not the only student who was not following directions. But he was the only one who responded disrespectfully.

10/25/19

Cornbread also got his school laptop taken away at school on 10/25 during a bullying assembly because he was playing Mindcraft, which is forbidden.

10/25/19

PW received a phone call from a California number at 9:37 am. The great grandmother on the mother's father's side called PW to tell him what was going on asked him why he was having her put in jail, which was a lie. He stated, I am not putting her in jail, she is 20k behind in child support and I do not have any financial means or power to do so. She is contesting the child support offices who have started the child support enforcement process against her for not paying child support. The great grandmother said, "you used to beat her" PW says ma'am, this is the United States of American and I am a black man. Do you think I would have full custody of my four kids if I were abusing her? You need to wake up and realize she has never taken responsibility for her life and she is lying to you. Great Grandmother said that the mother told her she has moved out of her mother's home and in with a friend, which we know is not true. The children's mother makes the rounds with phone calls to all relatives and will pay them money when he has it or call them to play the bleeding-heart mother who got her children taken away from her by her choices to abandon the children on several occasions.

10/28/19

Colleen told PW Davis that we received an e-mail from one of his teachers. It was received on 10/24. We have been busy getting ice, candles, and food from the massive storm that happened on Saturday and did not check e-mail.

10/28/19

Around 7 pm Colleen told PW about the incident at school and PW asked Cornbread not to lie. Cornbread proceeded to lie. This was the second time he has been disrespectful to a teacher at school. He was warned the first time. PW asked him to go to a bedroom to receive a spanking. Cornbread resisted several times and punched his father in the face 2x. PW did spank him. Afterward, a family meeting was called to discuss the negative and disrespectful attitudes in the home. It was a lengthy conversation full of clear rules, how chores need to be done, homework, etc. and telling the kids how smart and beautiful they were. The home motto is to be leaders, not followers, be your person. After many times of asking KK about some of the things his mother asks and has asked him to do, the following is below. In a former incident when KK was outside playing with an aerosol can and a lighter pointed at his face, he got in huge trouble due to the severity of the safety risk. The neighbor called PW, who was at work in Nashville over an hour away. PW said to tell KK to stop what he was doing, or he was going to whoop his ass. Based on this comment, the mother told KK to call the cops on his daddy for abuse. PW rushed home and when he got there, he explained to the police officer the dangers of what his son was doing and how he could have set himself on fire" Wouldn't you have threatened the same thing if this was your child officer?" The office agreed and left the scene. When questioned, he admitted that his mother told to him call the cops on daddy, then proceeded to tell KK in all in all incidents where he got in trouble at home to always call the cops on dad.

KK also said his mom tells him to delete all text messages from her

Princess admitted that her mom told her about the gun incident that happened last year with her and an unknown man she was with and told is she did not remember the incident where his mother was drunk and she had to take the booze bottle out of her hands.

11/9/19

PW Davis sent texts to the mother inquiring about when she was picking up the kids for Thanksgiving break. Also, Princess and KK called their mom from the home phone. Afterward, the behavior of KK became defiant, he spits in a bowl of ice cream and was not listening to Colleen when she asked him multiple times to clean up, put bowls in the sink, etc.; KK kept playing with the home security system and Cornbread messed with the thermostat. PW was working this day and had the kids listen to him on speakerphone about how they need to be leaders and not follow any direction to do bad things, even if told to do so by their mom. The mom called the home phone at 1:30 pm, 11/9/19, and hung up.

There is a gap in text messages from 10/29 to 11/9. The mother asked KK to delete text messages. She was trying to get our personal information out of a child.

11/13/19-Verbal attacks on PW and Colleen via text

The Mother:

"I have the right to speak to them and in privacy without you around to invade our conversations. And second of all you bitch can shut the duck (Fu**) of lying because I have not called and hung up multiple times. I called the other day no one answered, so I never called back and then I called before I called your phone a while ago and still no answer because she bitched and complaining to them when they were talking to me on the phone. She better just shut up when it comes to the kids talking to me because I am their mother, and she is not. I am not worried about her being your finance, it will not last long anyway because you let the last one did not and neither have any of your relationships. No one can ever replace me as their mother.

PW Response:

The home phone was acquired for extra safety in the new home. Also, you tell the kids to delete text messages which means you are telling them adult stuff, which is emotional abuse. You can always call the kids on the phone and they can call you. I have never kept you from your children. There is a reason I am the custodial parent. For all the claims of abuse, how come the judge ruled in my favor. With the injustices towards black men, I would be in prison for shoplifting like how you tried to teach our middle son how to steal from Walmart. Please stop your hostility. The kids answer the home phone freely. They may have been playing outside.

11/19/19

Text messages between Patrick and his ex-wife. She states, "That's what my child support pays for" and the money comes directly out of her checks.

11/28/19

Below are a few examples of suspicious actions that occurred. JC admitted that he requested remote access to our home security system when his dad was letting him play Pokémon on his phone. When asked if his mom put him up to that, he denied it

11/30/19

Received a letter from Sprint for an incomplete application for a cell phone plan. No adult in the home filled out any application. When PW asked Junior if he filled it out, he denied it, though was asking about the letter prior, told us it was nothing. PW called Sprint and the application was submitted on 11/2/19 and it came from a laptop with an IP address attached to the old Preston Drive.

12/2/19-Facebook Suspicious Activity

12/19/19

Cornbread had his mom on speakerphone and was excited and telling her what he had gotten from the rest of us for Christmas and he accidentally called her Colleen two times. She got livid and said "She is not your mom; you are not calling her mom, are you? The night before the drop off KK continued with disrespectful behavior and even chased after cats to harass them.

12/20/19

Colleen dropped the kids off at Walmart to meet their mom and when the mom greeted Cornbread it appeared that she chewed him out for something

1/6/20

There was no communication with us at all during winter break and the mom was late getting into Clarksville. Normally she drops them off between 12n-1pm. Both of us had to work and we said that Colleen would come to Walmart by 4:15. She refused, and we agreed she can drop the kids off at our mailbox on the street and not come to the front door.

1/11/20

Behavior from KK was significant while doing chores and room clean up. He took an end table that he and JC were sharing, moved to the side of the bed, and refused to get off of the table. Finally, after repeated requests of asking him to move, through yelling, he threw a fit and stomped off. Also, while walking the dog as a group, myself, Princess and JC, KK picked up a used diaper with a stick and later a decent size rock. I asked him to make sure he did not leave the rock in the middle of the road, because it would damage a car if they drove over it. We were walking and I had my back to him and suddenly a man stops his car and tries to get our attention. I am protective of the children and talk to the man at first, but after he asked a couple of times, he informed me that KK threw the rock and it almost hit his car. I apologized to the man and immediately reprimanded KK. KK smirked and claimed it was an accident and since I had my back to him, I did not witness it. I sent him home. KK also peed in the goldfish pond, even after Cornbread told him to stop. PW asked him about it when he got home, he lied about it and then PW said, I saw it on camera he called him out on it.

1/22/20

Received a phone call from Cornbread's math teacher regarding his disruptive behavior at the beginning and end of class. She tried to talk to him and said he shut down and would not tell him what was going on. I also received a call from his science teacher. She stated that he has been tardy 6x this semester, that typically they write students up after three tardy infractions.

1/26/20

Cornbread is failing Science, Math, and Social Studies. Colleen has helped him with homework numerous times, and he does not turn the paperwork in and blames the teacher or makes up excuses. He had been watching television all day. Colleen turned off the television and he reluctantly looked on Google Classroom and got nothing accomplished. She came downstairs frustrated and told PW. He told him we are not helping with homework anymore, it is on him to ask for help or start applying himself and if he gets held back, it is on him. Their mom called last night and again the wild disrespectful behavior began, including fighting over small things.

1/27/20

Cornbread's math teacher called Colleen at 237 pm informed me that Cornbread was bullying the kid behind him, kept threatening him with physical harm. She removed him from class, tried talking to him about the issue and he kept getting more elevated. Then in Homeroom at lockers, a kid came up to her and said Cornbread slapped him. She did not witness it, but she did see him do a shoulder check on another kid.

1/29/20

PW sent an e-mail to the assistant principle addressing Cornbread's behavior concerns and requested that the school start the process of alternative school. He never got a response to his e-mail, instead, she called him on 2/3/20 and explained that the mother called to the school and wanted information from her on Cornbread. When PW asked why he was not contacted until now he was given the brush off. When he challenged her with the fact that you drop everything to take a call from the mother who is not in their lives, and you do not call me, the custodial for a week, that is discrimination based on gender. She blew it off. The reason for the phone call prevents a paper trail so the school can cover its ass. Mom called Cornbread and said that he was not in the wrong for his behavior, proceeded to tell him that he needs 75 points to go to an alternative school. Later on, that night Cornbread was bragging that he only has 10 points and laughed at Colleen.

2/3/20

Colleen Davis called the assistant principal to discuss Cornbread's behavior. She spoke about "Daniel Tiger's Neighborhood, a storybook series to help kids handle their feelings. She spoke about a time when she saw Cornbread in class refusing to sit down after the teacher asked him to sit, then the assistant principal asked him to come to the hall and he huffed and puffed, gave him a chance to calm down, then asked if he was ready to talk. She then asked him if he wanted to act like a 6th grader or a three-year-old? She categorized his behavior as disrespectful vary and that he "Has his moments" and that teacher's tolerance levels for behavior Colleen then told her about his outbursts at home, how he threw punches at his father, puts a knife to other's throats as "play" Colleen explained that his mother is not in his life, there are abandonment issues and how one phone call from her demolished all the work we are doing with him. He has an F in four classes, despite our efforts on homework with him and us being involved. She did not seem overly concerned.

2/6/20

Cornbread started his in-school suspension, which is 4 days. Colleen gave him money to go to the dance that day at 2:30 pm. Colleen received a call from the school to pick him up at 3 pm. He bought a ticket, then a staff member told him, that because he was in school suspension, he cannot attend the dance, and if he gets caught, he will get kicked out and written up. He chose to sneak in and got caught. He received 2 additional days for this choice.

2/16/20

JC and Cornbread got into a huge fight over a power cord. At one point Cornbread told his brother, " I don't need a weapon to kill someone" Then he looked at me, snapped out of it, and said "I didn't mean that" KK and Cornbread continued the entire day with constant defiance and blatant disrespect. Cornbread refused to do any late homework again. Colleen kept encouraging him to do homework and then he got in her face as if he wanted to get into a physical fight. He finally backed down

2/17/20

Cornbread refused homework again. The whole day was spring cleaning day. KK and Cornbread only did their room with Colleen standing there the entire time to make sure the room got cleaned.

2/18/20

No School day. Cornbread and KK were disruptive all day. We were low on milk, so Colleen asked JC and KK to walk to the store and give me the change back. JC came back and omitted that he was thirsty and said that he got a beverage and KK convinced him to get him a cheeseburger and tried to get JC to lie to me and say that the milk was more expensive. This is a significant example of how influential their mother's behavior is in their decision-making process.

2/18/20

JC told his mom about Cornbread's grades and told me that she said she was not going to activate his phone or get him any birthday present until his grades were up. He was cooperative last night with homework. He talks a lot about wars, the apocalypse, and weapons.

2/28/20

Cornbread completed his extra credit project for the Science class on a poster board. He came into Colleen's office with his rolled-up assignment and he said catch this, so I did. She turned around for a second to add an item to our grocery list, then when she turned back, he drilled the tube into my eye/forehead. It left

a goose egg, bruise, and a cut. He did not have any impulse

control, even though he apologized.

3/1/20

PW called a family meeting to discuss the disrespecting, lying, not

picking up after themselves, and grades. Cornbread proceeded

with attitude and when his father talked close to his face, he

bucked up to him once again and slapped his dad multiple times,

and tried to wrestle him. PW was defending himself and was able

to get him retrained quickly. We both told them that all negative

behavior end tonight and rules and chore chart will be, followed

every day

3/14/20

Colleen came back from running errands and the house looked

like a disaster despite rules/chore list efforts and the dog pooped

in the house and the whole home smelled foul.

3/20/20

Challenges with visitation during COVID 19. Even though there were some restrictions, which were lifted she did not attempt to come to pick up the children for a visit. The same excuses were made regarding her finances, COVID 19 and her having the flu this winter.

4/11/20

The mother paid for one month of Minecraft subscription. She also paid for some of KK's Nintendo Switch games. No toiletries have been purchased or sent since they came back from winter break in January 2020.

4/16/20

Keyboard arrived from Amazon for Cornbread from his mother

5/23/20

Dropped all the kids off at 1 pm at Walmart. They spent the weekend with their mom in Nashville

5/25/20

We were supposed to pick Cornbread up at 1 pm at Walmart, however, she let the kids know that we had to be there at 11 am. She had changed the time. All of the kids got out of the car to say hello and we picked up Cornbread. We waited in the parking lot to make sure the other three children left safely. She waited in the same spot for over 30 minutes before she took off as if she were waiting to meet up with someone. We saw a suspicious car pull up next to her car, then it pulled away quickly.

6/13/20

The mother called the home phone at 9:12 am. I answered the phone and the conversation is below:

Colleen: Hello

Mother: May I speak with Cornbread

Colleen: No, Cornbread is at boy scout camp and will be back around 1 pm at the church

Mother: " No, I am picking him up

Colleen: Cornbread told us Sunday, June 14th. Then she went into a rant, acted restlessly and there was anger and urgency in her voice.

Mother: If PATRICK would keep me informed

Colleen: You need to text us the information, so we are clear on information, do you want to speak to Patrick

She raised her voice again, and I gave the phone to Patrick

Patrick: Informed her once again in a calm manner that she needs to give information to him, the adult because that is what she is supposed to do per the court order.

His ex-wife proceeded to yell at him, go on a rant, cussing him out, and called me a smart mouth bitch. She then called back multiple times. He did not pick up, because she chooses not to have a civilized conversation and we need everything in writing because she makes up stories and lies.

She sent multiple, texts which were full of anger. She then said she will meet us at Walmart at 2 pm, then that changed to 4 pm. Cornbread called her when he got back to our house, and he told her that KK and JC told him she was coming Sunday. She argued with him and said it was Saturday. She also arrived early at Walmart and did not give us notice. Cornbread's clothes still needed about 20 more minutes in the drier, but she stressed him out so much that he packed damp clothes. We dropped him off at Walmart on time. KK got out of the car, ran to me, and hugged me. He told me about all the new clothes that he had gotten. She glared at Colleen the whole time. Cornbread told us she got a new car. She did, it is a Honda Crosstour, moss green color.

7/6/20

The mother dropped the kids off late, though Princess notified her father using her mom's cell phone. Normally she parks far away, but this time she rolled up two parking spots next to us. KK and Princess got out of the car and hugged me, we chatted for a bit as the mother stared and glared at Colleen like usual. KK and

Princess decided to go back with their mom and not on our family trip to North Carolina. JC expressed to me the following. Her mom may be getting back on her feet, may move in with an old friend in Memphis or Atlanta, GA, but then said she cannot live in TN due to the business she had with their dad and collections. He also said, she would have received 10K more if she had wet or gone #2 in her car accident. She gave them $250 each for clothes, some cash, has a new car with Sirius XM in it, and put $3,000 down on it. She also told him that she gets food stamps because she is considered homeless, though at this time there is not a way to prove the information.

7/9/20

The fantasy continued for Princess and KK. They chose not to go on the family vacation to North Carolina. PW gave them the choice and has never made the children choose between him and their biological mother. Again, she chose to contact the children to let PW know when she was going to drop the last two kids off. She sent a text to PW the Friday before, though it was vague, and she did not mention time. JC kept telling Colleen that daddy is supposed to text mommy, that is how it is supposed to go. This drop off was different. Both Colleen and PW drove to Walmart. Their mom had a female friend with her this time. Princess started taking her items to the truck. Colleen said hello and she walked right by her and did not say one word. KK put on his best Hollywood cry performance for his mother and she held him, stroked his head, and comforted him. He stopped the tears quickly when he got into the truck. PW was getting ready to drive away. Their mother was on the phone and seemed to be cussing and yelling. The conversation ended and as he drove past, she did her usual stare and looked at PW with hateful eyes and glared at him. When they got home, the energy and family dynamics remained through the roof until bed. The arguments over petty things began and everyone assumed their roles within the dysfunctional dynamics.

9/25/20

Home dynamics reached a peak today. PW had a chore list to get the house in shape before possibly going on a day trip with the family. When Cornbread got off the bus from school, he asked his dad "Can I go to C's house" C is a troubled kid and is Cornbread's puppet master. He influences him into trouble all the time and has been forbidden to see him. The incident last fall, involving the PTSD neighbor, knocking on their door and running away was the icing on the cake, which also included repositioning the camera in the side of the house to not get caught. This sparked s series of arguments the entire day. Next, PW asked him to pick up his room and start cleaning, and Cornbread gave him attitude, took a swing, and bucked up to his father. He took matters seriously and was left with no choice but to wrestle him and spank him. This trickled on down to Princess coming home and immediately getting blasted to go clean the bathroom, which the two older boys continue to trash, urinate on the seat, and leave feces smears all over the toilet. JC took on his usual role of being fearful and got right into cleaning and when KK got home, he was told by Colleen to get right to work cleaning. PW asked all of the kids if they wanted to live with their mother after he explained to them "she abandoned you, never visits you, does not have a place for you to stay or financial means to support you, and lastly, "doesn't give a shit about you". With that said, and lots of tears, all the kids, except Cornbread said they wanted to stay here. Multiple abusive text rants from their mother, she is supposed to come to get him the next day. PW and his ex-wife had a heated argument and she called Colleen an old bitch and hung up the phone on him multiple times. PW knows she will not be able to handle him because he has the potential to knock her out and she will most likely call the cops. Colleen told him "leave it in God's hands"

CHAPTER 11 CONTINUOUS FIGHT

Even though there are ongoing incidents, the fight is worth it according to PW. The main goal is to keep the children safe, sound, happy, and hopefully successful. He often says the kids may or may not figure out who has been more stable for them, though will have to fall hard on their face and hit bottom before they understand what their mother has and will continue to put them through. He is not one to give up on fighting for his kids and has taken other avenues to get movement for his child support case. Mind you, she is now $20,000 behind on child support and both Tennessee and Missouri child support office told him, "We cannot do anything if she does not respond to our letters and disciplinary actions to get her to pay her court-ordered child support." If PW were the one not paying child support, he would have police officers at his door arresting him and hauling off to him to prison and most likely get roughed up physically by the police too.

Anyone who witnessed it the incident may assume and say, "Looks like another no-good piece of garbage black man going to jail." Is this fair to assume the scenario, yes, because black men are the most discriminated against in our society. Some of the action items include sending his ex-wife itemized expenses and a letter by certified mail for the children's expenses since she does not pay child support. The items are for school supplies, extracurricular activities, orthodontist bills for their daughter, and 50% of the food bill. He sends these packets by certified mail to ensure she gets the bills. She has acknowledged receipt of them, yet chooses to play games, work the system well and not support her children, which she is ordered to do. PW has met with several attorneys regarding his situation and they give him the same advice, its $1,000 to retain me, we can maybe get her 10 days in jail to scare her, yet there are no guarantees. He even sent out a letter to what were supposed to be father's rights attorneys, asking them if they can take his case pro bono.

The following is his heartfelt letter. He received one phone call back and nothing from the other law firms. It did not surprise him that he did not receive much response to his letter, attorneys must make a living and you pay for what you get, free representation. These types of workarounds do not discourage him or prevent him from living life or get him down, because he is a strong black single father who is determined to fight for what is right. The letter below is part of an endless effort to plead for help in his case, which has been an uphill battle for years.

February 3rd, 2020

I am writing to you with a heavy heart and mind. On July 24th, 2017 by the 3rd circuit court for Davidson County, Tennessee, I was awarded to be the custodial parent of my four children whom I had with my ex-wife. The court system typically awards the mother to be the custodial parent, not the father, and especially in my case, being African American is a unique situation.

I am financially drained because of the noncompliance of their biological mother. In the spring of 2016, she bankrupted the family and filed a tax return by claiming the children on the return. This choice forced us to get evicted and made us homeless and we lived in a Salvation Army homeless shelter for a few months. I barely financially support my four children through my job as a tenured electrician. I also work overtime and donate plasma to ensure they have food, clean clothes, and security.

The following are the areas where she is not abiding by the guidelines of the parenting agreement and breaking the law:

- Over six months behind on child support on January 30th, 2020 of $15,488.51
- Medical arrangement 60/40
  - On three occasions has taken the kids to the ER without notifying me
  - I am also listed on the bill as the caregiver
  - Braces account for our oldest daughter is behind over $700
- Does not inform the Child Support office of address or employer change
- Has not followed the visitation guidelines

Non-Custodial's History

- The Gun charge, though was dropped due to a plea bargain, she agreed to not see the kids for 6 months
- History of emotional abuse, including abandonment, manipulation, neglect
- Exposing the kids to alcohol and drugs, partying, and racism
- The unstable living arrangement, living with multiple families in a small duplex/home
- Tells adult conversation to kids, particularly our 9-year-old
- August of 2019 showed up in Clarksville and attempted to remove the kids from school
- Filing of false police reports on me
- Police have been at my home on several occasions because she tells the kids to call them

I have been doing the following:

- Calls to Child Support office to get updates
- Sending monthly certified letter/itemized bill to the mother for 50% of the children's needs
- Keeping the mother informed of any significant changes with the children
- Offered to get her set up in an apartment in Clarksville to be closer and she decided not to
- Documenting incidents, hostile text messages, Facebook posts and with the children
- Implemented restraining orders when necessary

I would be extremely grateful if you will choose to take my case pro bone. If I had enough financial support, I would have hired a family law attorney a long time ago. My case is special because I am a credible, hardworking, responsible, African American father doing my best to protect my children whom I love. If the situation were reversed, I would be in jail and required to pay child support.

Feel free to reach out to me with questions

He is doing his best to find a way to work around outdated laws, a sluggish child support system, and racial and gender bias towards single black fathers. Some days he does feel like giving up because of the court-ordered battle, which has been going on since May of 2017. He is mentally exhausted yet continues to go to work every day in a highly skilled trade on hot roofs in 100-degree heat and he can lose his life from a high voltage electrical shock at any moment. Is he still a lazy black man, who sags his pants and is a deadbeat father in your eyes?

Recently, he took a day off work and drive to an attorney who was 3 hours away. He is known for being fair, aggressive, and winning battles for custody in favor of the father when the situation involves a deadbeat mother. He recommended a revision of the parenting plan to be more specific. The non-custodial parent is not making her monthly visitation, which she demanded she has. She lives 9 hours away and chose to propose the third Thursday of every month for her to drive to pick up the kids. Two days are spent driving, leaving two whole days to spend time with them. Next, he said she is definitely in civil contempt for non-payment of child support and we can go after the amount, yet if she is not able to pay it, we do not know where she works, this makes things a huge challenge. Lastly, he recommended a private investigator to figure out her daily activities and see if she did get a settlement from a car accident and blew it all the money and still chooses not to pay her child support.

After leaving the meeting, he felt he got more clarity on the parenting order, however, continues to be in the same boat. The last item he acted on was moving the case from Davidson County in Nashville. In his experience, the court system is lenient for women and fathers have an uphill battle from the beginning due to their gender. He wanted to move the case to Montgomery County for convenience and the court system tends to be more conservative and upholds orders more, instead of caving into a white woman's fake sob story about her life and fake domestic abuse claims. In August of 2020, the case got moved from Nashville to a Montgomery County and he feels this may give his case a fresh set of eyes and actions. He remains cautiously optimistic and will begin to build a relationship with the new child support office.

As a black father, who is the custodial parent, he will still be seen as a "deadbeat" by most of society, though he stands firmly in his truth as a man, father, and husband, he knows the stereotypes he faces every day when he walks out the door into society. For the higher intelligence people who know about his situation, they already understand how rare it is for him to have custody due to his race and gender. They never even think to ask the question "what about the mother?" because they know how unique his situation is. For all others, it is a waste of his breath to give a laundry list of facts, incidents, and explanations to help them understand that mothers can be unfit to raise their children.

His life story does not have an ending or conclusion. Until legislation is changed, the media portrays black men positively and the law is upheld, he will always have to jumps through hoops and great lengths to make sure his kids are in a stable environment, which is secure and loving. The conversation he has had multiple times about their mother stealing from them and putting them all in a homeless shelter goes in one ear and out the other, because of the game she plays on them and manipulating them to think she is a supermom. PW feels the only way they may become awake is when they choose to live with her and become saturated in her environment, which is not suited for children to thrive in.

He has always taught them to be leaders and not followers and he prays one day they wake up and are thriving, following their dreams, and are happy. His life story continues to unfold and writes itself every day. He is currently seeking legal representation to assist him to take action to get the courts to take action for back child support and the mother not following the parenting plan. The intention of telling his story is to give a voice to single fathers, especially single black fathers who are going through similar circumstances of gender and racial bias regarding custody of their children.

PW is passionate about helping other single fathers navigate through the red tape and to keep fighting for their children, even when they feel there is no fight left in their soul. With all that he has been through with his family, he remains humble and grateful. He is always willing to meet their mother

halfway, yet until she can forgive herself, heal from her wounds,

and not focus on PW, the same dynamic will continue. Deep

down he wants happiness for everyone including the mother of

his children. The future is something which remains

unpredictable, his energy is focused on the now, he does not live

in the past with any regrets and makes the most of the present

moment. His faith in God has gotten him and his family through

turbulent times and he always states, "I love my life and God

loves me."

www.ingramcontent.com/pod-product-compliance
Lightning Source LLC
Chambersburg PA
CBHW072154090426
42740CB00012B/2265